The Horn of Africa

The SOAS/GRC Geopolitics Series

Territorial foundations of the Gulf states
EDITED BY Richard Schofield

The boundaries of modern Iran
EDITED BY Keith McLachlan

The Horn of Africa
EDITED BY Charles Gurdon

The changing face of the Balkans
EDITED BY Frank Carter & Harold Norris

Transcaucasian boundaries
EDITED BY John Wright, Richard Schofield, Suzanne Goldenberg

The Horn of Africa

EDITED BY

Charles Gurdon

School of Oriental and African Studies
University of London

UCL
PRESS

First published in 1994 by UCL Press.

UCL Press Limited
University College London
Gower Street
London WC1E 6BT

The name of University College London (UCL) is a registered
trade mark used by UCL Press with the consent of the owner.

ISBN:
1-85728-123-3 HB
1-85728-124-1 PB

British Library Cataloguing-in-Publication Data
A catalogue record for this book
is available from the British Library

Typeset in Palatino.
Printed and bound by
Biddles Ltd, Guildford and King's Lynn, England.

Contents

Preface

The publication of this edited volume by some of the foremost authorities in the region comes at an appropriate time because in the past few years the Horn of Africa, the collective name given to the countries of Sudan, Ethiopia, Somalia and Djibouti, has undergone a period of rapid and profound change.

The Islamic fundamentalist regime in Sudan, which came to power in June 1989, is not only advocating but also carrying out a series of radical measures in order to turn the giant heterogeneous country into an Islamic republic. It is unclear whether Sudan will remain a unitary state or will split into a predominantly Arab north and African south.

In January 1991 the Siad Barre dictatorship collapsed and today Somalia has split into at least two parts; while the north broke away when the Republic of Somaliland declared its independence in May 1991, the rest of the country has declined into a seemingly endless civil war. Given this continuing anarchy in the south, it is currently inconceivable that the people of Somaliland will willingly rejoin the rest of the former Somalia.

Meanwhile, the military defeat thatwhich led to the collapse of the Mengistu regime in Ethiopia in May 1991 resulted in the takeover in Addis Ababa of the Tigrayan-dominated EPRDF coalition government. Unsurprisingly, the unity forged in the common struggle against Mengistu soon disintegrated, and even without Eritrea's inevitable declaration of independence in April 1993, the centrifugal forces would have continued to gain strength. The government in Addis Ababa will struggle to keep what remains of Ethiopia as a single state. Meanwhile, these changes in neighbouring countries are spilling over into Djibouti, which had previously been a prosperous island of relative calm in a sea of poverty and disorder.

In Chapter 1 on "The effects of secession on Ethiopia and Somalia", Patrick Gilkes is highly sceptical about the benefits of the seemingly inevitable disintegration of the unitary nation state and analyzes the question of secession, the most significant issue facing the countries of the Horn of Africa today.

This is followed by Paul Henze's chapter on "The primacy of economics for the future of the Horn of Africa" (Ch. 2), in which he argues that strong economic links are the key to peace and prosperity in the region. In contrast, Alex DeWaal is far less optimistic, and in Chapter 3 on "Rethinking Ethiopia" he provides a detailed overview of the events in the country between May 1991 and the end of 1992 and then addresses the crucial issues of who are the contenders for power; the political process and the search for legitimacy; the economic crisis; and the resurgence of militarization in the rural areas.

Chapters 4 and 5 present two contrasting opinions on the former Somalia. Patrick Gilkes charts the terrible "Descent into chaos: Somalia January 1991–December 1992" in the south of the country. This is followed by a far more upbeat contribution by Gérard Prunier, the acknowledged French authority on the region, who in Chapter 5 provides a detailed analysis of the north's breakaway from Somalia, the creation of the new independent state and its future prospects while also touching on the effects of the Somali conflict on neighbouring Djibouti.

In Peter Woodward's chapter on "Sudan: a new political character?" (Ch. 6) it is the question mark that emphasizes his doubts. He argues that the radical measures taken by the regime that came to power in June 1989 are not so much an Islamic fundamentalist "revolution" but an intensification of processes that have been at work for a longer period. While the National Islamic Front (NIF) is geared towards gaining and consolidating power, and then perhaps spreading it to other countries, Woodward believes that the depths of its foundations in Sudanese society will remain comparatively shallow.

This is followed by a highly personal article on "Sudan's political and economic future: a southern perspective" by Bona Malwal (Ch. 7), who was minister of information in the Nimeiri government and is undoubtedly one of the most widely respected southern Sudanese politicians. As a supporter of John Garang's wing of the SPLA, he is deeply critical of the breakaway Nasir faction and argues that only the efforts of a united Sudanese opposition will rid the country of what he correctly views as the worst regime in Sudan's post-independence history.

Finally, in Chapter 8 the actual course of Sudan's political future during the next decade is forecast by Charles Gurdon, who believes that the current Islamic fundamentalist regime in Khartoum cannot survive more than a few years. While this will probably mean a return to the *status quo anti*, it is argued that the regime's overthrow will initiate a gradual change in leadership and, more importantly, the eventual separation of religion from politics.

It is not surprising, in a collection of papers by such a group of distinguished experts, that the authors do not always agree with each other and that, indeed, some of their opinions are diametrically opposed to those given by other contributors. There is no simple answer to any of the questions raised about the region's future, and so the debate continues. This is particularly true of the question of whether the best solution is secession and potentially independence or the maintenance of possibly artificial unitary states.

Contributors

Patrick Gilkes is a writer, broadcaster and consultant on Africa. He was formerly head of the BBC Somali Language Service, a producer with the BBC African Service, and a lecturer at Addis Ababa University. His publications include *The dying lion: feudalism and modernisation in Ethiopia* (New York: St Martin's Press, 1974) and *Conflict in Somalia and Ethiopia* (Hove, England: Wayland, 1994).

Charles Gurdon is Projects Director of the Geopolitics and International Boundaries Research Centre at the School of Oriental and African Studies, London, and the Managing Director of Menas Associates Limited. He is the author of *Sudan at the crossroads* (Wisbech, England: Menas Press, 1984), *Sudan in transition: a political risk analysis* (London: Economist Intelligence Unit, 1986), and has written for the Economist Intelligence Unit's Country Report for Sudan since 1983.

Paul Henze is a resident consultant at RAND in Washington DC. He has long specialized in the Horn of Africa and he travels there frequently. He has published many articles, reports and monographs on the economics and politics of the region. His most recent book is *The Horn of Africa, from war to peace* (London: Macmillan, 1993). He served as an observer in the Eritrean referendum in April 1993.

Bona Malwal is editor and publisher of *The Sudan Democratic Gazette*. Before his exile from Sudan, he was formerly Sudanese Minister of Culture and Information, and the Editor of the *Sudan Times*. He has recently been a Senior Research Fellow at St Antony's College, Oxford. His publications include *People and power in Sudan* (London: Ithaca Press, 1980), *A second challenge to nationhood* (New York: Thornton Books, 1985), and *Sudan: a drift towards separation* (New York: Lilian Barber Press, 1994).

Gérard Prunier is a senior researcher at the Centre d'Etudes Africaines in Paris. He is the author of *From peace to war: the southern Sudan, 1972–1984* (Hull: University of Hull, 1986), *l'Ouganda et la question indienne, 1896–1972* (Paris: ERC, 1990), and co-editor of *Les ethnies ont une histoire* (Paris: Karthala, 1989).

Alex de Waal worked as Associate Director for Africa Watch for three years before leaving in December 1992 with his colleague Rakiya Omaar to set up the London-based Africa Rights organization. His publications include *The famine that kills: Darfur, Sudan, 1984/5* (Oxford: Oxford University Press, 1989), *War in Sudan: an analysis of conflict* (London: Peace in Sudan Group, 1989), and *Evil days: thirty years of war and famine in Ethiopia* (London: Africa Watch, 1991).

Peter Woodward is Senior Lecturer in Politics at the University of Reading. He is author of *Condominium and Sudanese nationalism* (London: Rex Collings, 1979), *Sudan, 1898–1989: the unstable state* (Boulder, Colorado: Lynne Rienner, 1990), and *Nasser* (Harlow, England: Longman, 1992); he is editor of *Sudan after Nimeiri* (London: Routledge, 1991).

The Horn of Africa, 1994

CHAPTER ONE
The effects of secession on Ethiopia and Somalia

Patrick Gilkes

Two new states, Eritrea and the Republic of Somaliland, established *de facto* independence in the Horn of Africa in 1991. Irrespective of their recognition, or indeed of their survival, their respective struggles had marked effects. The collapse of the regimes of Mengistu Haile Mariam in Ethiopia and of Siad Barre in Somalia can be directly, if not exclusively, related to the guerilla activities of the Eritrean People's Liberation Front (EPLF) in Eritrea and the Somali National Movement (SNM) in northern Somalia. Certainly their wars against the central governments, for whatever reason, were major factors in weakening, beyond repair, the highly centralized regimes that have now collapsed in both states.

There are certain arguments that follow from this fact, but any discussion depends upon the reality of the nation and the state and an understanding of what a nation actually is.[1] One approach, largely prevalent in the Horn, has tended broadly to follow Hegel and Stalin in what has been called the "genetic view", which emphasizes that individuals in a nation share, *inter alia*, culture, history, language, race, religion, and territory. This has been seen as particularly true of Somalia and of Somalis, but it also underpins much of the recent nationalist writings from the Oromo, Afar thinking, the Ethiopian People's Revolutionary Democratic Front's (EPRDF) decision to base the Council of Representatives in Addis Ababa on ethnicity, and the current stress in Ethiopia on the concept of self-determination.[2]

Another view of nation is that it grows out of historical and economic processes and that its boundaries are the consequence of social and political activity. In other words, individuals join groups for their own advantage. This allows both individuals and groups to reorganize their allegiances as necessity dictates to form a state around one ethnic group, as did most western European polities.[3] This of course provides a much more dynamic view of the nation, although, in the context of the Horn, it has a certain irony. It allows for a realistic interpretation of the Eritrean struggle, because under this argument the colonial experience creates a reason for people to rethink historical alliances. Equally, it allows a reality to the historic Ethiopian nation within current boundaries, something the "genetic arguments" would essentially contradict.[4]

1

This second view can be called the "political creation" of national ideology, elaborating identity and differences which together can determine a national continuity. It implies a collection of ideas and beliefs which may, or may not, have historical foundations for political reasons. The political dimension is, in fact, a critical element and one that can be adjusted. A striking effort to adjust the ideology of the state came in the 1970s and 1980s when the Ethiopian state rejected its Amhara–Tigrayan feudal class traditions as the centrepiece for national identity and tried to substitute socialism and a worker–peasant class alliance as the basis for a "progressive" state. A recent study of 20th-century Ethiopian peasant revolts concludes that Ethiopian peasants were stirred to revolt by economic inequalities, political injustices and cultural denials and not by ethnic divisions.[5]

This raises questions about the creation of nations in the Horn of Africa. Is it inevitable, or even desirable, that various nationalities should become nations or, to carry the argument further, nation states? Is there any reason why Somalis should form a single nation state? Frontiers need not be unchanging, nor require natural boundaries. Both have been flexible in the past. The creation of the Republic of Somaliland falls within the development of what one might call subnationalism among Somali clans as it is mainly, if not exclusively, the preserve of the Issaq. There are other possibilities. The Majerteen, for example, have a longer and more centralized history than most Somali clans.[6] The Ogaden, in the aftermath of Ethiopia's 1978 defeat of Somalia, made it quite clear that their appeal to self-determination did not necessarily include their incorporation in the Somali state – a view that brought some Western Somali Liberation Front (WSLF) leaders into conflict with Siad Barre.[7] Even the Somali nationalist hero, Mohammed Abdullah Hassan, the Sayeed, appealed as much to Islam as to Somali identity, and his relationship with other Somali clans was frequently antagonistic.

The question of the Oromo is obviously relevant. There has been an upsurge of discussion on Oromo history, culture, the right to self-determination and the concept of Oromia in recent years.[8] Some of the five main Oromo groups now speak of the need for an independent Oromo state, and with the present government's stress on self-determination these ideas are rapidly gaining wider currency. Oromo history, of course, can be interpreted in alternative ways to the current emphasis on a crushed and colonized people. In the 16th century the Oromo overran much of the highland areas of the Amhara and the Tigrayan peoples. Many became agriculturalists and were assimilated to a greater or lesser extent. Subsequently, in the 17th and 18th centuries, the Oromo were one of the three main nationalities involved in the Gondarine Empire, the others being the Amhara and the Tigrayans. Power fluctuated between these groups and between leading individuals from these peoples. For example, the family of the Oromo Ras Ali the Great was locked in conflict with the house of Ras Michael Sehul of Tigray for much of the period between 1770 and 1850. Control later passed through various regions including Tigray before ending up in Shoa in the latter part of the 19th century. Oromos constitute the largest single ethnic group, and they have every political incentive to preserve and democratize the present Ethiopian polity.

Another group with political aspirations are the Afar who now live in Ethiopia, Djibouti and Eritrea. Those in Ethiopia clearly want and expect self-determination. Some of those in Djibouti are currently fighting the regime, less with the aim of trying to split the country or break away than of trying to democratize the current regime. Nevertheless, the creation of an Afar state in Ethiopia, however impoverished, might well have an appeal to Djibouti's Afars, particularly if such a state could acquire control of southern Eritrea and the port of Assab and thus the transit trade to Ethiopia. Faced with an external Afar state of whatever description, any Eritrea will have to make it more attractive for Afars to stay within Eritrea. In the context of self-determination in the Horn of Africa, this may prove to be difficult. The EPLF cannot afford to continue with what appears today to be a flat dismissal of Afar claims that Eritrea's Afars are Eritreans. As one Afar leader has put it, "the EPLF fought for 30 years to achieve self-determination; we would hope they would look on our claims with respect."[9]

The EPLF's own success essentially arises from the fact that the repression of Haile Selassie and then Mengistu Haile Mariam, in particular, made the Ethiopian state so unattractive that an historic element of that state, the Tigrayan population of south central Eritrea, preferred to opt for withdrawal under any circumstances rather than stay within the central polity. In its wider sense, the history of the creation of the Eritrean liberation movement and its success emphasizes the point that a nation is defined by economic and political processes. Eritreans do not have culture, language, race or religion in common; no multinational state does. What they do have is a colonial experience which was highly successful as a boundary-defining exercise. The anti-colonial struggle does not challenge the existence of the colonial state or its rights over the colonially defined and recognized territory or population. It was the question of control that was the issue.

Eritrean nationalism would also appear to be a recent, and in some ways artificial, phenomenon. The reality of the EPLF's anti-colonial claims against Ethiopia and the rejection of the word "secession" demonstrates a deliberate confusion between a conflict caused by a state's oppression of minorities and an external power's suppression of a colonial population. This is the basis of the largely fictitious history of Eritrean nationalism, for which there is no evidence before the Italian period and very little prior to the 1960s. Indeed, Eritrean nationalism appears to have remained a minority interest until the mid-1970s.[10] This does not affect its validity or, in any way, deny the reality of the struggle. It does, however, suggest that Eritrean nationalism is a late development, in particular among the region's Tigrayan population. Tigrayans were, of course, a people whose history, economy, culture and religion were linked into the rest of Ethiopia and who largely supported union throughout the 1940s to 1960s. The peripheral northern and western areas, the home of pastoral nomadic populations, were another matter. They were rarely, if ever, under imperial influence. It was there that the struggle against central power began, and there that it was confined for the first decade.[11]

After 1952 the central Ethiopian government certainly imposed an essentially Amhara culture on Eritrea. Whether this can be translated as "colonialism" is open to question. Imperial central government control was not accompanied by the confiscation of land as it was in the south in the late 19th century. Cultural assimilation and social mobilization are normal elements in the creation and activity of any state. It is when the latter exceeds the former that you see the rise of ethnic nationalism, which tends to arise from the effects of urbanization and commercial and industrial growth rather than exploitation. Economically, Eritrea between 1962 and 1974 was the most favoured region of Ethiopia after Shoa, and by 1970 it had over one-third of the country's industrial activity. Although Shoa had nearly 50 per cent, the next largest concentration was in the Harerghe region which had less that 10 per cent. This is not saying very much. During the federation the economy was steadily run down. In part, this was due to the emigration of businessmen and technicians, particularly Italians, and the loss of their capital and expertise. Another cause was the struggle between the Eritrean authorities and the Ethiopian federal government for control of the Eritrean economy.[12]

What took place in Eritrea after 1952 was essentially part of a trend towards centralization imposed by Emperor Haile Selassie after 1941 throughout Ethiopia. At first at least, resistance to it owed more to the struggle against despotism than to anti-colonialism. The importance of anti-colonial elements is that an end-product is independence, and it is from this perspective that the Eritrean issue becomes of political significance. The EPLF's insistence on the colonial element is not just a critical factor in buttressing Eritrean nationalism; it is equally important for its future relationship with the Ethiopian state, with which it will presumably have close links. (Ethiopia is the natural hinterland of Eritrea, just as the latter is the natural outlet for Ethiopia.) In fact, Eritrean independence need not affect the existence of an Ethiopian polity. The domino theory is not a certain end result, attractively plausible though it may be. Nevertheless, the EPLF–TPLF alliance and the EPRDF's subsequent acceptance of Eritrean claims and its decision to opt for an ethnic solution to the crisis of the Ethiopian state does raise the possibility of disintegration in Ethiopia as another of the periodic reactions to over-centralization that have occurred throughout Ethiopian history. This is made more plausible by the EPLF's theory of anti-colonialism, which has provided the Oromo with the possibility of a similar approach.

Equally, it can be argued that the EPRDF's approach is no more than a realistic variant of the political solution that was in theory favoured by the previous regime: that of regional autonomy (i.e. the restructuring of the Ethiopian state on democratic norms and on the basis of self-determination). The EPRDF has accepted, albeit somewhat uneasily, the EPLF's determination to opt for independence, but it is clearly hopeful that this will not be repeated by the Somali, Afar or Oromo, the three other regional groups most likely to make such an attempt.

The full details of the EPRDF's vision of Ethiopia have yet to be clarified, but it will involve 12 autonomous regions with Addis Ababa and Harar having special status. This allows for the Afar, Agau, Amhara, Oromo, Somali and Tigray to have their own regions. Most of the other regions will have multiple ethnic representation, and the government expects a number of coalitions to become active. The political and economic relationship between these regions and the central power has yet to be decided but the key element, as among most of the parties represented in the Council of Representatives, is ethnicity.

Northern Somalia has perhaps as good a case as Eritrea for independence. It has a separate colonial history under the British, with the south being controlled by Italy. Somalis were also subject to the French in what was to become Djibouti, the British in the future state of Kenya and the Ethiopians in the Ogaden. In British Somaliland politics centred around the Somali National League (SNL), created in 1947 from the Somaliland National Society, which, in turn, had grown out discussion clubs in Berbera, Buro and Hargeisa in the 1930s. Both were founded on the basis of unification of all Somalis and on a pan-clan concept. By the late 1950s there were two main parties in the British Protectorate, the SNL and the United Somali Party (USP). They took the north into union with the south in July 1960, six days after northern independence, but they appeared ambivalent about it from the start. The consensus over future relations with the south was reached only after furious debate before the idea of an immediate union was acceptable. The first government of Abdul Rahman Shaermarke was a coalition of the Somali Youth League (SYL) in the south and the SNL and USP in the north.

The first test was the referendum in June 1961 for the new constitution, and many SNL strongholds in the north campaigned against it in order to "safeguard northern interests", despite the fact that the party was in the coalition government. In December 1961 a group of Issaq junior officers attempted a coup, though this appears to have been less a clan reaction to unity than a quarrel over the spoils. In 1963 the coalition collapsed. In the next few years political wheeling and dealing, leading to northern leader Mohammed Ibrahim Egal joining the SYL and becoming prime minister in 1967, did little to allay northern feelings that they were being neglected. It was a feeling that only increased during Siad Barre's regime.

A critical factor in the growth of northern discontent was the Ogaden war. Somalia's defeat was followed by the refugee crisis of the Ogaden, with hundreds of thousands crossing mainly into northern Somalia.[13] This was followed by the appearance of the Somali National Movement (SNM) in 1980. Its subsequent cohesion, though fragile, meant that it could become a vehicle for northern interests in a way that the predominantly Majerteen Somali Salvation Democratic Front (SSDF) failed to do in the central areas because of internal divisions.[14]

The debate over secession surfaced in the SNM as early as 1981 and, although the SNM constitution clearly underlined the real need for the preservation of Somalia's territorial integrity, the secessionist wing remained powerful as it was to prove in 1991. It was based on a widespread appreciation of Siad Barre's failure to develop the north, or rather, his efforts to impoverish and perhaps destroy it.[15]

Recent events suggest that Somali nationalism remains segmentary and it appears that pan-Somalism is unlikely to be revived in the near future. The Somalis in Djibouti and northern Kenya are obviously separate. The north appears obdurate over its declaration of independence and the Ethiopian regime accepts self-determination for the Ogaden area. Given the chaos in southern Somalia, it seems unlikely that the region will include Somalia as an option. The creation of the Republic of Somaliland will take the resolution of Somali irredentism a stage further. It is likely, once the Organization of African Unity (OAU) can force itself to accept the concept, that Kenya and its allies, including the United States and Britain, will back Somaliland for that very reason.

There is no longer any superpower strategic rivalry at risk. Secession will have little or no effect on the region. In so far as there is a strategic dimension, in the wake of the Soviet Union's collapse, it is regional, with the Arab–Israeli conflict figuring prominently. In this context the only real change is that two new players have entered the game and will effectively substitute superpower rivalries along the Red Sea littoral for Ethiopia and Somalia, both now cut off from direct involvement. It is not clear which way Eritrea and Somaliland will move on the international level, but both have indicated a strong desire not to become enmeshed in any wider confrontations and both can be expected to put a high price on any political alliance. However, the two new states do offer the possibility for considerable wheeling and dealing in terms of local Red Sea alliances.

In Africa there have been three strands of state activity. First, there is the highly centralized and often, though not invariably, colonial state; frequently imposed from outside, this is based on a territorial definition and has the goal of territorial nationalism. Second, there is the ethnic community created by history and culture and giving rise to ethnic nationalism or, on the downside, tribalism. Third, there is the continental approach of pan-Africanism which is equally indigenous.

These levels of activity can conflict as they have done in recent years in the Horn. (Equally, they can co-exist in what have been defined as "concentric circles of allegiance".) Despite the recent history of the Horn, there is no necessity for conflict between them. Nationalism has all too often become the main ideological vehicle for the intelligentsia to stake their various claims to leadership, and this is where conflicts often arise.

Whatever pattern of states or nations emerge, the importance of creating a viable economy has even greater significance. Paul Henze has argued this case to leaders in Addis Ababa "to create conditions of rapid economic growth, a rising standard of living and an open society in which Ethiopians could exercise their talents for enterprise and self-expression" as a means for ending dissidence and allowing a vigorously developing Ethiopian state to become a model of prosperity for the region.[16] Although the political scene has moved on considerably, the point of his analysis remains valid. Without real economic incentives, a free market and an enterprise economy, the development of a pluralist and democratic society in any part of the Horn is unlikely. With them, the options are considerable and the question of secession within, for example, an economic community of the Horn of Africa, an irrelevance.[17]

Notes

1. On the question of state formation in Africa, see Anthony D. Smith, *State and nation in the Third World* (Brighton: Wheatsheaf Books, 1983) and I. M. Lewis, "Pre and post colonial forms of polity in Africa", in *Nationalism and self-determination in the Horn of Africa*, I. M. Lewis (ed.), 67–76 (London: Ithaca Press, 1983).

2. Mengistu's regime also used Stalin's definition of a nation, accepting, in theory, the right of self-determination while rejecting any realistic right to secession. See J. Stalin, *Marxism and the colonial question* (London: Lawrence & Wishard, 1936); V. I. Lenin, *On the national and colonial questions* (Peking: Foreign Language Press, 1967)

3. C. Tilly (ed.), *The formation of national states in western Europe* (Princeton: Princeton University Press, 1975).

4. Smith, p. 124. Both Ethiopia and Eritrea, like all African states except Somalia, Lesotho and Botswana, fall into the category of "polytechnic state based territorialisms".

5. Gebru Tareke, *Ethiopia: power and protest: peasant revolts in the 20th century* (Cambridge: Cambridge University Press, 1991).

6. L. V. Cassenelli, *The shaping of Somali society: restructuring the history of a pastoral people 1500–1900* (Philadelphia: University of Pennsylvania Press, 1982).

7. J. Markakis, *National and class conflict in the Horn of Africa* (Cambridge: Cambridge University Press, 1987).

8. Mohammed Hassan, *The Oromo of Ethiopia: a history 1570–1850* (Cambridge: Cambridge University Press, 1990); B. K. Holcomb & Sisai Ibssa, *The invention of Ethiopia: the making of a dependent colonial state in north east Africa* (Trenton NJ: Red Sea Press, 1990).

9. Personal communication.

10. Tekeste Negash, *No medicine for the bite of a white snake: notes on nationalism and resistance in Eritrea, 1890–1940* (Uppsala: University of Uppsala, 1986). For alternative views, see Okbazghi Yohannes, *Eritrea, a pawn in world politics* (Gainesville: University of Florida Press, 1991); Jordan Gebre-Medhin, *Peasants and nationalism in Eritrea* (Trenton NJ: Red Sea Press, 1989).

11. Markakis, p. 104–31.

12. Between 1952 and 8 the number of industrial establishments fell from 400 to 74; by 1974 the number rose to 165, about 35 per cent of Ethiopia's total capacity.

13. I. M. Lewis, *A modern history of Somalia: nation and state in the Horn of Africa* (Boulder, Colorado: Westview Press, 1988).

14. D. Compagnon, "The Somali opposition fronts", *Horn of Africa Journal* **13** (1990).

15. Saeed Sheikh Mohammed, "Siyad's vendetta against the north", *New African* (September 1987); Amnesty International, *Human rights abuses and civil war in the north* (London: Amnesty International, 1988).

16. P. Henze, *Ethiopian economic prospects for the 1990s.* RAND (N–2857-USDP) (Washington DC: RAND Corporation, 1989).

17. There are encouraging signs of efforts to tackle some of the problems (e.g. agricultural development, nomadic pastoralism, Nile waters, access to ports) on a regional basis.

CHAPTER TWO

The primacy of economics for the future of the Horn of Africa

PAUL HENZE

Introduction

The first section of this chapter reviews the recent past in Sudan, Ethiopia and Somalia in addition to focusing on the present problems and future possibilities, particularly for Ethiopia. Political and security conditions in Sudan, and especially in Somalia, have so deteriorated that it is impossible to do more than discuss future economic possibilities in terms of general principles. Ethiopia, in contrast, has undergone a healthy transformation from Dergue (military junta) rule and is experimenting with policies that facilitate rapid recovery. Ethiopian politics, however, could develop in directions that would negatively affect economic development. The Transitional Government of Ethiopia (TGE) in Addis Ababa and the Provisional Government of Eritrea (PGE) in Asmara are pursuing quite different political courses. Both stress their commitment to the free market and privatization of much of the economy. Both are likely to be more successful if they can find a basis for economic co-operation and reduction of potential causes of political friction.

The legacy of authoritarian regimes

The legacy of two decades of authoritarian rule in all three major Horn countries is almost entirely negative.[1] The recent rulers of these countries – Jaafar Nimeiri and his successors in Sudan, Mengistu Haile Mariam in Ethiopia and Siad Barre in Somalia – claimed to be motivated by a resolve to speed up the pace of modernization and economic development. In reality, they all gave priority to consolidating their own power and forcing their highly diversified countries and societies into a single, dogmatic social, economic and political mould. They all used force to suppress movements seeking regional autonomy.

9

All three leaders fell victim to the Soviet Union's willingness to supply arms and its inability to provide economic assistance or effective economic advice. Economies lost momentum, and were hindered by unproductive expenditure. As more and more economic activity went underground, both tax and customs revenue fell. Agricultural mismanagement, intensified by drought, led to famine, as confiscatory delivery requirements discouraged production for more than local needs. Bureaucracies became more and more corrupt, infrastructures were neglected, and more and more educated and technically qualified personnel emigrated or fled. Although the quality of life deteriorated in all Horn countries during the past two decades, the population continued to grow at a relatively rapid pace. Millions of people became refugees, sometimes several times over. A significant proportion of the population in all three countries suffers from malnutrition and chronic disease. Many still suffer from shortages of food and other basic needs. Unemployment and underemployment have increased. Educational standards have fallen, and resources available for education and social services, already meagre, have contracted.

Both Somalia and Sudan continue in a downward spiral of political and economic deterioration. In Ethiopia, however, the tide appears to have turned. The country faces formidable problems of recovery from the mismanagement of the Dergue, but the leadership of the Ethiopian People's Revolutionary Democratic Front (EPRDF) has committed itself to the establishment of a genuinely democratic political system, an open society and a free market economy.

The Transitional Government of Ethiopia has dissolved Mengistu's deceptively named Workers' Party of Ethiopia (WPE) and his huge armies and renounced the use of force to maintain the country's unity. It has acknowledged the autonomy of the Provisional Government of Eritrea in the country's northernmost province, where Mengistu sacrificed hundreds of thousands of lives and squandered billions of dollars' worth of military equipment in futile efforts to force the population to submit to his rule.

Ethiopia's political recovery and return to economic health offer promise for the rest of the Horn. Since Ethiopia shares many characteristics with the other Horn countries, its current experience can become an example for Sudan and Somalia to follow

The lessons of Ethiopian socialism

Ethiopia's encounter with Soviet-style Marxist socialism devastated the country. The ideological base on which Mengistu built his people's republic was shallow and shaky. Mengistu had little interest in political or economic theory. Neither did most of his Dergue associates. Early Dergue officers, who had a more intelligent grasp of the realities of the late 20th-century world, were purged or exterminated during the first bloody years after the 1974 revolution. Many of the politicized leftist intellectuals who originally supported the Dergue fell out during the murderous infighting of 1975-8. Mengistu chose Soviet-style socialism because, first, it legitimized the exercise of power in the name of the "broad masses" while excluding them from all meaningful participation in political processes; secondly, the Soviets were ready to supply military aid unconditionally; and thirdly, he assumed that by aping the Soviet economic and social system he would be guaranteed development assistance. He was persuaded that the Soviet system represented the wave of the future in world politics; he was blind to its political sclerosis and economic failures.

The Soviets were much less eager to embrace Mengistu than he was to join their club. The entanglement with Mengistu's Ethiopia was always to some degree controversial in Moscow. Mengistu's best friends were hard-line gerontocrats and senior military officers – men such as Romanov, Zaikov, Chebrikov, Kryuchkov and the conservative generals, men who were incapable of acknowledging the economic bankruptcy of the communist system.

Mengistu skilfully manipulated his relationship with Kremlin leaders – including Gorbachev, who seems to have had little fondness for him – to secure a steady flow of arms and military supplies. Thus, looking back at the three basic reasons why Mengistu aspired to a close Soviet relationship, we can see that he was tactically correct in respect to the first two but very wrong about the third. In the end, the relationship led to his undoing.

Economic development mattered less to Mengistu than power and military support. At a time when the communist regimes of eastern Europe were experimenting with economic reform and when, even in the Soviet Union, the rigidities of "developed socialism" were coming increasingly under question, Mengistu chose to build a Stalinist economy, including state control of industry, tight regulation of domestic and foreign trade, and a regimentation of the agricultural population in state farms, resettlement sites and collective-style villages. It was a recipe not for modernization, but for stagnation and retrogression.

Because of their professed Marxism-Leninism, the insurgent movements that now hold power in Ethiopia were originally susceptible to many of the same economic and political delusions that proved fatal for Mengistu. As the 1980s progressed, both hard experience and a readiness to learn from it began to turn them into pragmatists. Rejection by the Soviets inclined them towards a critical evaluation of the Soviet and East European experience. More rapidly than Mengistu, the insurgent leaders drew relevant lessons from the crisis into which the Soviet Union began to fall in the 1980s and shed their illusions about socialism.

The process of disillusionment with the Soviet system occurred more rapidly among the members of the Tigrayan People's Liberation Front (TPLF), the dominant element in the EPRDF, than among those of the Eritrean People's Liberation Front (EPLF). To succeed on the ground, the leaders of both movements realized that they had to earn the support of the people they lived among and on whom they depended. They learned a great deal from administering regions that they wrested from Dergue control. Thus, by the time they took formal control of government in June 1991, they were ready to apply new political and economic policies. They had a catalogue of Dergue mistakes and Mengistu's failures at hand to serve as examples of what not to do.

Harsh reality

Mengistu fled the country on 21 May 1991, leaving behind a demoralized rump government that rapidly lost what little control it retained of the police and military forces. When the EPRDF came into Addis Ababa at the end of the month, it found the treasury almost devoid of foreign exchange and the domestic revenue system barely functioning. Most industry was operating at 25 per cent capacity at best. The transportation system was limping. Petroleum supplies were almost exhausted and the situation was complicated by EPLF takeover in Assab and the flight of its port personnel. Imports had almost ceased during the final months of Dergue rule. Highways and communications facilities in the northern third of the country were severely damaged by fighting. Millions of people continued to exist on emergency famine relief. War and civil unrest affected the eastern and western border regions.

The new leadership found that levels of corruption in the civil service, in service organizations and in the police force exceeded its worst expectations. Police and security services were suspended and large numbers of former officials and political activists were interned. Fortunately, the population of the capital was ready for peace. With a minimum of force, the EPRDF was able to deploy its fighters to maintain order and ensure continuation of elementary services.

The most odious features of Dergue rule were officially abolished, though the EPRDF had no alternative but to keep most of the central administrative structure intact. Its first priority was to create the framework for a transitional government with some democratic legitimacy. Within a month of taking power, the EPRDF convened a national conference in which a wide range of domestic political and ethnic groups, as well as some organizations in exile abroad, were represented.

The EPRDF conference created an 87-member council with many of the features of a legislature and produced a national charter embodying principles for the restructuring of Ethiopian government and society along democratic lines. EPRDF leaders sought to avoid friction with the EPLF -led Provisional Government of Eritrea in Asmara. This was not easy. Difficulties over Assab persisted despite an agreement that it would function as a free port for all of Ethiopia. The EPRDF had no alternative but to continue austerity policies by reducing imports, but European Community members provided quick emergency backing to ensure petroleum supplies.

The weather favoured the new government's aims, and throughout most of the country summer rains were heavy. The EPRDF encouraged speedy agricultural recovery and rapid increases in food production by allowing farmers to plant, cultivate and sell as they pleased, free from government controls, and by not restricting private trade in grain and basic agricultural products. Prospects for the 1991 harvest were therefore excellent.

The EPRDF-led Transitional Government of Ethiopia was criticized both internally and from abroad for not moving fast enough in devising comprehensive economic policies and creating a new political structure. New cabinet appointments were not announced until 11 August 1991, and the most important single post, that of finance minister, was filled only later in the month. Preliminary talks with the World Bank did not begin until mid-September.

EPRDF leaders in general, and President Meles Zenawi in particular, defended themselves by saying that they needed time to learn and wanted to be sure they were selecting competent people to form a cabinet which would have a significant degree of ethnic and political balance. They were also concerned with maintaining a good working relationship with their coalition partners, especially the Oromo Liberation Front (OLF).

Thus, while the TGE has still not received high marks from the Ethiopian public or from foreign observers for speed and efficiency, it has been commended for its openness and readiness to learn, for its determination to introduce a genuine democratic spirit into Ethiopian political life, and for its avoidance of dogmatic pronouncements on economic and social issues.

As early as the second week of July 1991, after only five weeks in power, President Meles engaged in several hours of informal television debate with several prominent intellectual critics. The contrast with Mengistu's arrogance and Haile Selassie's paternalism was lost on no one, and Meles won high public praise for fostering a deeper understanding of the principles the EPRDF is trying to implement. If Meles and the team he has gradually assembled to lead Ethiopia into a new era of freedom, democracy and prosperity and maintain, capitalize and build on this favourable beginning, prospects for Ethiopia are promising.

Political challenges

A good beginning is, however, no guarantee of successful accomplishment. Ethiopia's new leaders have generated high expectations and face formidable demands. The country has no experience of democracy to draw on, as some of the eastern European and a few of the former Soviet republics escaping from communism have. Authoritarian habits, traditional attitudes and limited provincial horizons still characterize much of the population.

The damage done by Marxism-Leninism may not be as great as in eastern Europe and the former Soviet Union. Ethiopian peasants have not forgotten how to farm, nor workers to work. Corruption, selfishness and ethnic resentments run deep, however, and with the opening up of society, many suppressed attitudes and grievances are emerging and causing strain.

Cleaning up after the Dergue is a challenging task – how to deal with party activists, former regime officials and military officers who have been guilty of crimes? So far the EPRDF has been careful to avoid summary justice, random vengeance and arbitrariness. It deserves credit for its respect for basic human rights and due process. But it is increasingly criticized by Ethiopians who suffered from Dergue abuses for treating internees too leniently, and by others for the delay in dealing with these people. Ethiopians are becoming accustomed to expressing themselves without fear of retribution – so groups are organizing, demonstrating and petitioning. The clamour threatens to boil over and threaten a govenment which is still consolidating its power.

Everyone in Ethiopia, from its leaders to peasants in the remote fringes of the country, has to learn that democracy can never be an end in itself. It is not something that, once achieved, remains in a steady state. It is a method for accommodating to change and solving problems, preferably through elections and orderly processes of discussion and decision-making.

Ethiopians are now discussing procedures for holding elections and operating political parties. Elections must take place in a political and administrative framework that will establish workable governmental structures and satisfy public expectations. The EPRDF is determined to give regional authorities greater power and responsibility. Federalism as a principle for holding this ethnically and geographically diverse country together is much talked about but remains to be implemented.[2]

Some aspects of the EPRDF programme have already aroused disquiet. One is its apparent desire to give ethnicity absolute priority in the administrative restructuring of the country. There is fear that ethnic conflicts that may be unleashed will prove uncontainable. There is also concern that this preoccupation with ethnicity may interfere with rational decision-making relating to economic development. EPRDF leaders argue that resentments and aspirations which have long been suppressed need to be aired to initiate a healthy process of reconciling differences and bringing Ethiopians to a realization of the advantages of voluntary union. Optimists hope that rational calculation of economic advantages will mitigate ethnic strains.

The difficult problem of devising a workable political party structure on an ethnic basis alone, given the country's great ethnic diversity, remains. As Christopher Clapham has recently argued, a completely ethnically restructured Ethiopia will contrast sharply with an Eritrea organized on different political principles.[3]

Some Ethiopians would like to see the TGE less passive in respect to Eritrea, for they are reluctant to accept Eritrean independence as a foregone conclusion. Attitudes range from a stubborn refusal to recognize that nothing but persuasion could keep Eritrea attached to Ethiopia, to the more rational argument that the issue should be opened for public discussion both in Eritrea itself and throughout Ethiopia.[4] There is a fairly widespread feeling that Eritrea should simply be written off as lost through Haile Selassie's mismanagement of the federative arrangement and Mengistu's subsequent brutality. This latter view is often, but perhaps incorrectly, attributed to EPRDF leadership.

Those directly concerned in the matter of Eritrea include hundreds of thousands of Eritreans long resident in other parts of Ethiopia. They are one of the most economically important components of the population of Addis Ababa. Before the referendum took place in April 1993, Eritrea, under its EPLF-organized Provisional Government, appeared to be undergoing a somewhat different political evolution from the rest of Ethiopia, though it is too early, perhaps, for a clear direction of development to have become apparent.

Some observers believe they detect residual Marxist attitudes and socialist sentimentality in both Asmara and Addis Ababa on issues such as land tenure and governmental management of some important economic functions, such as the control of exports. What in actuality seems most characteristic of both the TGE and the PGE leaders is their lack of rigidity and their readiness to examine issues, consult the people and evolve approaches that may differ fundamentally from the principles they advocated when they were guerrillas in the field. The TGE's Draft Economic Programme, which was subject to public discussion for several weeks, illustrates the new approach.

Leaders may be evolving much faster than some of their followers. However, followers too, are undergoing basic changes of attitude under conditions of peace and with new responsibilities weighing heavily upon them. These processes are not new in the world. They have been taking place among revolutionary and guerrilla movements for a long time. What is new for Ethiopia is that they are taking place in a sharply changed international context. The illusions about command administrative, political and economic development and fraudulent claims of representing the true interests of the people that were encouraged by the Soviet Union, by communist China and lesser Marxist–Leninist states (e.g. Tito's Yugoslavia) lie shattered beyond repair. They have no place in a serious programme for democratization and modernization. The Free World offers no pat formula for just systems of government and economic progress, but it has experience that has proved valid and principles that are adaptable to many different circumstances. The leaders of the new Ethiopia have made it clear that they wish to join the Free World. They also understand that they cannot achieve any of their goals without its support. So they have both an idealistic and a pragmatic justification for pursuing their chosen course.

Economic rejuvenation

The reluctant reforms that Mengistu decreed in spring 1990, and then backed away from, provide a base from which the far more comprehensive EPRDF policy of economic liberalization can evolve and take full effect.[5] The north-central regions of the country, freed of Dergue controls as EPRDF forces advanced, began a very limited recovery in 1989 and 1990.

Rapid agricultural rehabilitation is crucial for Ethiopia. The country must begin to generate income from exports. Coffee, always an important export crop, came close to being the sole source of foreign exchange during the Dergue period as production of other traditional export crops such as pulses and oilseeds declined and the government lost control of the livestock trade. Ethiopia's greatest resource is its manpower. Regimented, frustrated and discouraged from producing, Ethiopia's population became a burden, for it was unable to feed itself.

The TGE has sought to maintain wholly co-operative relations with foreign relief organizations in order to ensure the flow of food and relief supplies to avert famine. At the same time, it is co-operating with these organizations in their efforts to convert emergency relief into development assistance.

The basic TGE approach to agriculture is to leave the farmers alone and to encourage production and trade in agricultural commodities. With favourable weather, this approach could make Ethiopia largely self-sufficient in food within two to three years. Given the opportunity, the rural population can be expected to achieve a great deal of basic rehabilitation through its own efforts, including the restoration of smallholdings, the repair of roads and trails and the improvement of fields and water channels.

With the knowledge that they can profit from their labour and the assurance of land tenure, farmers will exert themselves to improve plantings of tree and bush crops. As development assistance becomes available, extension services and inputs of many kinds – fertilizer, improved seeds and tools – can be provided to farmers on an ever broadening scale. With an approach to agriculture that is helpful but non-intrusive, Ethiopia can enjoy indefinite and steady improvement in agricultural production of all kinds. Here, as well as in many other respects, the experience of India during the past four decades is a good example.

Ethiopia's great reserves of manpower are best kept on the land. There is, therefore, little justification for the expansion of mechanization for most forms of agricultural production. Restoration and improvement of degraded land in the highlands, improvements in storage and application of water and elementary inputs that enable farmers to raise production on existing fields are likely to prove more rewarding than bringing new land in remote regions under cultivation.

Mengistu's forced resettlement schemes wasted a great many resources, offended the highland peasantry and left very many enterprises in difficulty most of which will be best abandoned or scaled back drastically. State farms have, almost without exception, proved to be a heavy burden on the state budget and a poor method of increasing production. They must be rapidly privatized, broken up and redistributed to local farmers, or else abandoned.

Ethiopia offers broad opportunities for many kinds of specialized agricultural production – including fruits and vegetables, oilseeds, spices, garden seeds and flowers – that could be attractive to innovative local investors as well as foreigners.[6] Conditions also favour specialized livestock and poultry operations and fish farming. A plentiful and trainable labour supply is an important incentive for labour-intensive undertakings. Domestic food production is the most important priority for Ethiopian agricultural development, but agro-industrial production will be a natural source of additional agricultural activity. Food processing for domestic use and export also has an enormous potential for expansion.

Ethiopia already has a well developed textile industry capable of great expansion and assured of a large domestic market as the population acquires purchasing power. The country's enormous livestock herds, which already sustain exports in live animals, hides and skins, need to be upgraded. They are a source of supply for food processing and leather manufacturing industries. Ethiopia already has a productive sugar industry with considerable potential for expansion. Neighbouring countries in the Middle East are a natural market.

Economic rejuvenation in Ethiopia has in fact already begun and can continue simply on the basis of letting everyone – farmers, traders, craftsmen and manufacturers – do what they can with whatever is at hand. However, outside assistance is essential because the country was left strapped for resources by Dergue mismanagement and the distortions brought on by sacrificing all other considerations to pursuit of the civil war in the north. Africa has fallen to a relatively low priority among international lending institutions and donor countries. Ironically, the countries that authoritarian leaders used to regard longingly – and illusorily – as sources of assistance, i.e. the USSR, Eastern Europe and China, are now all competitors not only for development aid and investment, but also, in the case of the former Soviet Union, for famine relief.

Nevertheless, good policies and promising potential leave Ethiopia in a position to compete. EPRDF leaders seem well aware of both the opportunities and the constraints that they face. The TGE signed a preliminary agreement with the World Bank on 18 September 1991. The World Bank followed up with a mission in November to evaluate the state of the Ethiopian economy and requirements for a recovery programme. Major donor countries and the European Community have also sent survey missions, the outcome of which appears almost certain to be positive.

The Draft Economic Programme has focused public attention on economic issues. Assistance for the rehabilitation of the infrastructure, agricultural development and the restoration of industry will start flowing to Ethiopia during the coming months. It will be conditional on rational economic policies, sound financial management, the creation and maintenance of favourable provisions for domestic and foreign investment, expansion of democracy and improvements in provisions for enforcing social justice and ensuring the protection of human rights. There is no longer any support for governments that refuse to approach economic development rationally.

The multiplier effect

Once set in motion, economic growth feeds on itself. Ethiopia's experience can serve as an example for its neighbours. The fact is that, even during the past decade of acute authoritarian mismanagement and consequent deterioration of the economies of all three major countries, extralegal and informal trade (i.e. smuggling) between them has flourished, and borders that central governments have been unable to control have proved economically porous.[7] This trade has its good and its bad sides. It demonstrates that there is a greater rationale for trade between these countries than official statistics would justify. It demonstrates also that political, tribal and ethnic antipathy need not be a serious barrier to fruitful economic interrelationships. On the negative side, extralegal trade means a substantial loss in customs and tax revenue to the governments concerned. While few regretted these losses to unpopular and oppressive governments, the problem becomes serious, as in Ethiopia now, when a constructive government needs the revenue, which, among other things, can be applied to improving infrastructure and facilities to support increased trade.

Groups accustomed to operating outside the law acquire a vested interest in maintaining the "privileges" they have taken for themselves. Considerations of this sort appear to lie at the root of some of the unruliness that has afflicted Djibouti, eastern Ethiopia and northern Somalia. It is to be hoped that, with patience and determination, informal traders can be persuaded that their interest lies in co-operating with authorities whose ultimate intentions are constructive.

Service industries not only offer great promise for expansion but also have a high potential for generating co-operation among Horn countries. Several Ethiopian state corporations survived Dergue mismanagement, maintaining their autonomy and emerging both strong and capable of expansion. These include the Electric Light and Power Authority (EELPA), the Telecommunications Authority (ETA), the Highway Authority (EHA) and Ethiopian Airlines (EAL).[8]

All of these service industries suffered losses, but they maintained their integrity and efficiency because they had originally been set up in such manner as to preserve the autonomy of their management. As they were already state corporations, Mengistu could not nationalize them, but neither was he able to interfere decisively in their management. He did, however, restrict their efforts to expand and caused them to divert resources to support his military operations. Nevertheless, all have emerged from the Dergue era with their competence intact and are now expanding operations to serve the new Ethiopia's development priorities. They stand as examples for Ethiopia's neighbours to emulate and have the potential to assist them, when conditions become favourable, in their own development efforts.

To take an important example, Ethiopia's hydroelectric power potential is, according to some estimates, 98 per cent undeveloped.[9] The Blue Nile supplies up to 80 per cent of the vast flow of water that sustains Egypt. Its tributaries represent one of the world's richest potential sources of hydro-power. The water can be used for power with only limited effect on Egypt's water needs, as the Blue Nile and its tributaries flow in deep canyons, mak-ing its use for irrigation almost impossible. The Blue Nile terrain, however, favours the construction of dams to generate power. With systematic devel-opment, Ethiopia could supply power not only to satisfy most of its own steadily growing needs, but also to export power to Sudan and Egypt, or even the Arabian peninsula. The Blue Nile system is far from the only hydropower source in Ethiopia; the Webe Shebelle and other southern rivers represent a potential that Ethiopia and Somalia could share.

Ethiopia has no developed petroleum sources, although there are promis-ing indications which could be investigated seriously under peaceful condi-tions. Oil prospectors discovered major petroleum deposits in Sudan in the 1980s, but work on exploiting them came to a halt because of civil war. Under peaceful conditions, Sudanese petroleum could benefit all Horn countries and lay the basis for co-operative development in all aspects of energy production. Sudan's hydropower potential is also very high. Two dams on the Blue Nile supply a large share of the country's current needs.

Transportation is another field in which all Horn countries can reap great benefits from co-operation. At present, highway connections between them are primitive; better highways would facilitate legal trade. EAL, which serves neighbouring countries, provides trans-Africa services that far exceed those of any other African or international airline. Its capacity to expand to provide services for the commercial and government sectors is practically unlimited. Given peaceful conditions in Ethiopia, it has the capability to support a rapid expansion of tourist services, one of the most readily available sources of foreign exchange.

With continued internal peace and modest investment in existing infrastructure to support tourism, Ethiopia can expect to increase tourism revenue to Kenya's level in less than a decade and thus make it a major source of foreign exchange earnings. Ethiopia has a more varied range of attractions for tourists than any other African country. EAL, with its proven managerial capability and with the capital it generates from its profits, not only has the means of servicing international and domestic air routes but also could expand into tour operations and hotel management. For specialized tourism – such as helicopter flights to remote regions, monasteries and historic sites – it would be a natural and logical choice for developing specialized subsidiaries.

Eritrea

Eritrea represents a major development opportunity. It was the most highly developed region of Ethiopia, with more than a third of the country's industrial base. Moreover, it possesses the highest proportion of educated and trained manpower of any region except, perhaps, the central province of Shoa.

Along with southern Sudan and northern Somalia, Eritrea has suffered more severely than other regions of the Horn from authoritarian oppression and civil war. The damage has been greatest in Eritrea because there was more infrastructure to destroy. Mengistu's bombing of the port of Massawa after it was captured by the EPLF in February 1990 stands as one of the worst examples of vengefulness in a region that has seen too much mindless destruction during the past two decades. Nevertheless, prospects for Eritrea's recovery and transformation into one of the economic bright spots of the entire Horn of Africa and Red Sea region are judged to be good.[10]

In the spring of 1991 the leadership of the EPLF was persuaded to avoid a declaration of independence and defer a popular referendum on the question for two years. Several factors influenced this decision: (a) the likelihood that Eritrean independence would not be recognized by any major Western country and would not be welcomed in most of Africa; (b) the fact that recognition by radical Arab countries would not be beneficial from the viewpoint of basic Eritrean interests; and (c) the concern of the EPLF leadership that Ethiopia, freed of the Dergue, should evolve peacefully and constructively – an evolution on which a unilateral declaration of independence would have a negative influence.

There were strains between the EPLF Provisional Government of Eritrea and the EPRDF Transitional Government of Ethiopia, for the PGE was originally reluctant to accept any arrangement that would give symbolic substantiation to its continued subordination to the Ethiopian state. The rapid expulsion and departure into Tigray and Gondar provinces of defeated Dergue soldiers and their dependants, as well as central government employees and non-Eritrean civilians, placed a heavy burden on the new EPRDF authorities, the Ethiopian Red Cross and foreign relief agencies. The EPRDF leadership went to great lengths to minimize friction with the PGE and to contain the potentially troublesome Afar issue. With the passage of time, many points of friction have been minimized, but there is still a potential for strain and all the more so as Ethiopian society becomes more open and democratic with various groups expressing themselves in media and in terms of political action.

The Eritreans' desire for independence is understandable in light of the 17 years of brutal mistreatment that they have experienced at the hands of the Dergue.[11] The psychological and political case for independence appears weaker, however, if Ethiopia is democratically governed on the basis of a federal system with a high degree of regional autonomy.

Geographic and economic realities all argue for an extremely close relationship between Eritrea and Ethiopia. Eritrea would appear, in fact, to gain more from close association with Ethiopia than Ethiopia would lose from separation. With free trade, free movement of people and full economic cooperation, both will develop more rapidly.

Eritrean industry needs Ethiopia both as a source of raw materials and as a market. It can benefit from the services that experienced Ethiopian corporations, with substantial numbers of Eritreans among their personnel, can provide. Ethiopia needs Eritrean talent, skills and access to the sea. Economically, it is difficult to envisage any benefit for Eritrea in separation. The PGE's insistence on symbolic independence delayed arrangements for aid and investment and complicated financial relations, since Eritrea still used the Ethiopian *birr* as currency.

Goodwill and objective calculations of economic realities may have defused some of the tensions from the Eritrean issue. The political referendum that took place in April 1993 and met international standards for fairness and objectivity was an overwhelming vote for independence. The result is that Eritrea, politically and economically, is moving successfully towards not only an independent, but also a pluralist state.

The large numbers of Eritreans abroad have accumulated capital and acquired skills which could be put to good use in an economically expanding Eritrea or in other parts of Ethiopia. Will they come back and bring their money with them? Eritreans who live in large numbers in other parts of Ethiopia also possess capital and skills of great value. The TGE has been careful – in spite of occasional calls for discriminatory actions – to permit no pressure or threats of retribution against persons of Eritrean origin in retaliation for actual or alleged expulsions from Eritrea of non-Eritrean Ethiopians.

Several hundred thousand Muslim Eritreans have taken refuge in Sudan over the past two decades. Many were not originally EPLF enthusiasts. For the time being, Eritrea suffers from unemployment, but as economic momentum builds, these refugees will be a natural and welcome source of agricultural and industrial labour. Even without employment possibilities, many, given deteriorating conditions in Sudan, have expressed a desire to return to Eritrea. Where will they stand politically when they do? None of these Eritrean problems appears unmanageable, but they cannot be ignored, nor can they be contained by force if they become exacerbated. They represent a serious challenge for the PGE and to a lesser degree the TGE. If they are amicably and constructively dealt with, and, above all, if economic considerations are given priority by all sides, then all will benefit. If the political status of Eritrea in relation to the new Ethiopia can be arranged so as to produce maximum economic advantage – whether through recognition of political independence or by some other formula for autonomy that would allow Eritreans to play a vigorous and constructive rôle in respect to the whole country – a precedent applicable to the other divided and sorely tried countries of the Horn might be created.

Conclusion

The Horn of Africa has been poisoned by politics and devastated by military operations for more than two decades. If the leaders of the countries of the region are genuinely motivated by a desire to benefit their people, then it is time for them to define more important priorities and implement them. Economic momentum can reduce ethnic and social tensions. Dismal as conditions in Somalia and Sudan now appear, the region has at last been brightened by a new spirit in Ethiopia and Eritrea. If it prevails, and if all the country's new leaders can work successfully together, not only Ethiopia but the entire region will benefit and move towards a time of peace and progress in the 21st century.

Acknowledgements

With the support of RAND and the National Endowment for Democracy, I spent five weeks in Ethiopia in June and July 1991 at the invitation of the new government and observed its assumption of power firsthand. A summary of my observations was published as a RAND paper, *Ethiopia in 1991: peace through struggle* (RAND P–7743 1991, Washington DC: RAND Corporation). My book, *The Horn of Africa, from war to peace*, was published by Macmillan Press, London and St Martin's Press, New York, in 1991.

Notes

1. I say "almost" because, of course, some construction and some investment in infrastructure did take place. Sudan successfully explored for petroleum and began work on the Jonglei Canal. Ethiopia established some assembly and manufacturing facilities and educational institutions, such as the Agarfa Agricultural Training Centre and the Water Technology Institute in Arba Minch. Such institutions can be adapted for future use. Roads, irrigation installations and port facilities constructed in Somalia and Ethiopia during the past two decades also represent net gains for their economies, as do some urban buildings, housing developments, and storage facilities. Such gains, however, must be weighed against the deterioration in infrastructure from lack of maintenance, overuse and destruction during the fighting that has ravaged all Horn countries and continues in Somalia and Sudan. Factories set up along Soviet lines were sometimes poorly designed and often equipped with outdated machinery. A net assessment of gains and losses resulting from authoritarian rule in all three Horn countries would probably show substantial material losses, as well as less tangible losses in terms of time, opportunities, talent and resources.

2. India, an ethnically diverse country comparable to Ethiopia, offers experience that Ethiopians could productively study. It is organized on a federal basis with a substantial degree of recognition of ethnic preferences. It has never been free of frictions leading at times to communal violence. India has repeatedly had to resort to central government rule in the face of persistent violence or breakdown of authority in some of its states. This possibility has yet to be faced in Ethiopia and will need to be taken into account in the country's new constitution.

3. See , "The political destruction of Ethiopia and Eritrea" (1991). The EPLF acknowledges that Eritrea is a multi-ethnic society and recognizes nine ethnic groups. These include three which together may account for 40 per cent of the Eritrean population, and which have larger numbers in Ethiopia than in Eritrea: the Tigrinya-speaking highland Christians, who are identical to the Tigrayans of Tigre; the Afar, who inhabit the Eritrean panhandle; and the Bilen, an Agau group closely related to the Agau of Wollo and Gojjam. While, with the exception of the Afar, there is no current evidence of sentiment for ethnic unification, the experience of ethnicity in other parts of the world demonstrates that the possibility of such attitudes developing in the future cannot be ruled out.

4. Extreme adherents of the first position, more vocal among exiles in America and Europe than in Ethiopia itself, condemn the United States for having "given away" Eritrea in the course of the fast-moving discussions and contacts that resulted in recognition of the assumption of power by the EPLF in Asmara and the EPRDF in Addis Ababa in May 1991. They failed to understand that Mengistu's brutal 17-year effort to bring Eritrea to heel – an effort that ended on clear battlefield victory by the EPLF – "lost" Eritrea. These same critics, who also condemn the United States for having "brought to power" the EPRDF in Addis Ababa, ignore the fact that the EPRDF was able to enter the capital because it had waged a long war against Mengistu's forces and won. It was the combined effect of the EPLF and TPLF-EPRDF struggle that defeated Mengistu's far larger and better equipped armies. The United States was irrevelant to this process until a very late stage and during the final denouement had only a marginal impact. It sought to avoid Mogadishu-style destruction and carnage in both Asmara and Addis Ababa – i.e. to help the winners, the EPLF and EPRDF, peacefully take control. The populations of both these capitals were grateful that American political intercession in Addis Ababa and London led the collapsing Dergue remnant government of Tefsaye Gebre Kidan and Tesfaye Dinka to recognize the futility of trying to foment violence and resistance.

5. I observed the effect of these reforms in parts of the centre and south of the country in November and December 1990. When I described what I had seen to Mengistu in the course of a long meeting just before I left Ethiopia in mid-December, he seemed disappointed to hear that the population had seized upon the opportunity to leave the villages, plant freely and exploit the opportunities that open markets had begun

to offer. See Paul B. Henze, *Ethiopia in 1990: the revolution unraveling* (RAND P–7707, Washington DC: RAND Corporation, 1991).

6. *Veronia galamensis*, an unusually productive oilseed that grows in marginal areas and is well suited as an auxiliary cash crop for individual farmers, was discovered by a US agricultural scientist in Hararge about 25 years ago. Efforts to encourage its cultivation during the Dergue period failed. It is now being commercially produced elsewhere in Africa and in Latin America and offers good potential for Ethiopia.

7. The same has been true in large part of borders of Kenya and Uganda and, to some extent, of sea trade between Ethiopia, Djibouti and Somalia with Yemen. Djibouti has been a major focal point of all this trade and has functioned, in fact, as the hub of an informal Horn of Africa free trade area.

8. *The Economist* featured Ethiopian Airlines in a 1987 series on successful enterprises in seemingly hopeless countries; see "In search of excellence, the hard way", 26 December 1987. EAL's experience was also highlighted in a *Financial Times* account in summer 1989. See also the airline's account of its own history, *Bringing Africa together* (Addis Ababa: EAL, 1988).

9. There is only one hydroelectric power installation on the Blue Nile system in Ethiopia – the dam below Tisisat Falls east of Bahr Dar.

10. I sketched out a vision of an economically flourishing Eritrea as a "Switzerland" of its region in a talk to Eritreans for Peace and Democracy in Baltimore, Maryland, in November 1990.

11. There is as yet no objective measure of attitudes of Eritreans on this question and little basis for judgement on how opinion may be evolving.

CHAPTER THREE
Rethinking Ethiopia

Alex De Waal

Contemporary Ethiopia is thoroughly confusing. It is difficult enough to catalogue the events of the past few years, let alone make sense of them and hazard predictions as to what will happen next. This is partly because the changes of May 1991 represented an earthquake in the political landscape that destroyed the old certitudes which were perhaps highly misleading anyway. Just as the new rulers of Ethiopia are professing a political reinvention of the country, it is necessary for observers to rediscover the nature of the political forces they are dealing with. This chapter is a tentative attempt to identify some of the issues that warrant consideration, prior to writing a contemporary political economy of Ethiopia.

Following a cursory overview of the main political events between May 1991 and the end of 1992, this chapter addresses four important sets of issues: who is contending for power; the political process and the search for legitimacy; the economic crisis; and the resurgent militarization of the countryside.

An overview of events since May 1991

The victory of the combined forces of the Ethiopian People's Revolutionary Democratic Front (EPRDF) and the Eritrean People's Liberation Front (EPLF) was a moment of high drama. The final battles were fought while US-sponsored peace talks were being held at the Berkshire Hotel in London, and by the time the conference concluded the EPRDF were in control of Addis Ababa. This coincidence has led conspiracy theorists in Ethiopia (of whom there are many) to conclude that the EPRDF victory was an American plot. This is of course an absurdity: if anything, the diplomatic intervention of the State Department under Ambassador Herman Cohen served to slow down rather than hasten the advance of the EPRDF. The EPRDF and EPLF had won the war in February and March following an extraordinarily violent and protracted struggle over the previous decades[1] and it only remained for the former government of President Mengistu Haile Mariam to acknowl-

25

edge that fact. Mengistu gave a *de facto* admission of defeat by fleeing the country for Zimbabwe on 22 May 1991, but such was the state of ignorance in which other levels of government and the general public of Addis Ababa were kept that many Ethiopians fail to acknowledge the military realities to this day. Meanwhile, the Oromo Liberation Front (OLF), having failed to anticipate the military success of the final EPRDF-EPLF offensive, found its military position marginalized.

In convening the peace talks, the agenda of the United States included permitting the emigration of Ethiopian Jews (Falashas) to Israel, facilitating famine relief in the north of the country and thereby lessing the cost to USAID, and avoiding an urban bloodbath like that witnessed in Somalia earlier in the year. The United States also hoped to persuade the EPLF to accept a federation with Ethiopia. Strategic and commercial interests were insignificant. During the course of the conference, both military events and the dramatic evacuation of almost all the Falashas by Israel changed the agenda. The Ethiopian army was defeated and Eritrean independence became a *fait accompli*, which Cohen was obliged to accept. Instead, the US administration found itself negotiating the government's surrender and committed itself to supporting a democratic experiment in Ethiopia.

In accordance with the agreement reached at the London talks, a national political conference was convened in Addis Ababa on 1 July 1991. This witnessed the highest degree of political pluralism ever seen in Ethiopia. The conference adopted the Transitional Charter, a document enshrining the Universal Declaration of Human Rights, and promises of democracy and self-determination for the Ethiopian nationalities.[2] Following the adoption of a permanent constitution, it promised swift regional elections followed by national elections by the end of 1993. An 87-member Council of Representatives was established, including 32 EPRDF representatives, 12 from the OLF and a range of others chosen from various smaller liberation fronts and ethnic groups. Meles Zenawi became president of the Transitional Government. Shortly afterwards, a cabinet was formed consisting of a spectrum of members of the liberation fronts and technocrat individuals who were considered untainted by the crimes of the former government. The EPRDF reserved the key posts of prime minister, foreign minister, defence and internal affairs for itself.

The EPLF did not participate in the July conference, and instead established a Provisional Government of Eritrea (PGE), consisting exclusively of EPLF members, to prepare for a referendum on the issue of independence in two years' time. Eritrea is now independent.

Meanwhile, drought relief, rehabilitation and the demobilization of Mengistu's defeated army were established as priorities for the Transitional Government of Ethiopia (TGE). The adoption of an economic policy was secondary, but this was delayed both by difficulties in finding a finance minister and long debates in the Council of Representatives. The establishment of the national regions was also delayed, because of long discussions over how the boundaries should be drawn and the regional councils constituted.

The transitional timetable was overtaken by events, in particular by military clashes between the EPRDF and the OLF in the southeast. The London talks had agreed that the liberation fronts should continue to administer any territory they already controlled before Mengistu's defeat; other areas were to be under the authority of the EPRDF. In the southeast, the OLF claimed to have liberated large areas, while the EPRDF claimed that these areas had been under the control of the former government. This issue became academic, as during August there were escalating attacks on EPRDF troops, in garrisons and convoys, throughout the southeast, chiefly by OLF forces. It is questionable how well controlled these forces were, and there is evidence of a split in the OLF between the more conciliatory Deputy Secretary General Lencho Leta and the more confrontational Secretary General Galassa Dilbo.

The first of a series of EPRDF–OLF agreements was negotiated in late August 1991. This provided for EPRDF control of the main towns, roads and economic installations and for OLF withdrawal to rural areas. Almost simultaneously, the Council of Representatives (including the OLF representatives) voted to make the EPRDF army the national army for the transition period.

The August agreement failed to stick, and conflict soon broke out again in the east. Not only was the OLF involved, but various other Oromo, Somali and Afar groups also fought each other and the EPRDF. In addition there was widespread banditry and many inter-ethnic clashes. Similar problems also surfaced in other parts of the south.

Regionalization, the centrepiece of the government's programme, was repeatedly delayed. The 14 new regions were announced only in December 1991. The proclamation was largely the work of the OLF. Meanwhile, slow progress was made on economic deregulation, re-establishing a police force and a functioning judiciary and other administrative matters. In early 1992, disagreements led to the resignation of the "technocrat" Ministers of Justice and Finance.

In late 1991 and early 1992 a series of agreements were struck between the EPRDF and the OLF, of which the most important was mediated by the EPLF and agreed at Meqele in Tigray on 18 February 1992. *Inter alia*, this provided for the encampment of both parties' forces prior to the holding of regional elections and the creation of local dispute-resolving committees, each with representatives from the EPRDF, OLF and EPLF. This also met with only uneven success. Conflicts continued and the rhetoric on both sides became more vehement. Each side accused the other of bad faith; the EPRDF accused the OLF of unprovoked attacks and breaking agreements, while the OLF accused the EPRDF of becoming another army of occupation. Fighting and talking continued, consuming most of the government's energies. On the whole, the EPRDF maintained the upper hand militarily, partly by failing to honour its commitment to encamp its forces, though the OLF remained able to mount guerrilla attacks throughout much of the south.

On 20 June 1992, the much delayed regional elections were finally held in most parts of the country. Three days earlier, alleging widespread intimidation, the OLF announced that it would boycott the elections, and withdrew from the government. The elections went ahead, scrutinized by international observers who later reported that the elections were deeply problematic, and could not be considered competitive in most areas. Threats of a large-scale OLF offensive coincident with the elections failed to materialize.

The crisis over the OLF withdrawal momentarily appeared to plunge Ethiopia to the brink of civil war. To date, this has not happened. This was due partly to the military unpreparedness of the OLF, and partly to new rounds of negotiations, this time convened by a group of Western ambassadors. Both OLF and EPRDF, contemplating the abyss, appeared to take a step backwards. As well as welcoming the negotiations, the government convened a Commission of Inquiry into electoral malpractices, opening the door to a compromise that would allow the OLF back into government. It also promised to reconsider the question of the formation of an integrated national army. However, in August 1992 it filled the ministerial posts left vacant by the OLF withdrawal.

After several postponements, the elections in the Afar and Somali regions were held and also saw widespread malpractice although EPRDF surrogate parties failed to take power. Throughout the rest of the 14 regions, the EPRDF and its surrogate parties controlled the government, although their degree of popular support is highly questionable.

Throughout the second half of 1992, the government engaged increasingly in practices reminiscent of an authoritarian regime, rather than one dedicated to democratic transition. There were mass roundups of ethnic Somalis, kidnappings of refugees from Sudan, bans on opposition organizations, intimidation of dissenters and the internment of large numbers of alleged members of the OLF and other organizations that were suspected of planning anti-government violence. In January 1993, this culminated in the violent repression of a student demonstration in Addis Ababa, which coincided with the visit of UN Secretary General Boutros Boutros-Ghali. At least seven students died when the police opened fire, and the University of Addis Ababa was then closed.

The contending forces

The three main blocs contending for power are the EPRDF, which chiefly represents the north but also a number of other categories; the Oromo nationalist bloc (including the OLF and others); and the "centralists", who have traditionally controlled the state. In addition, there are numerous marginal or small groups, mainly in the south.

For the north, controlling the state is an economic imperative, because Tigray and the adjoining areas are so impoverished and environmentally degraded that there is no alternative source of sustenance. In Tigray, even staple foods are provided by international aid channelled through parastatal organizations. For the Oromo and other southern peoples, the rôle of the state has traditionally been to extract wealth from them; they have prospered most when the state has been weakest. The representation of Oromos in government has, until 1991 at least, failed to alter this aspect of the state. Hence an ambivalent attitude towards the state is characteristic of the south: should the state be appropriated, or destroyed? The "centralists", who are mostly but not exclusively Amhara, share with the northerners the need to control the state, though for different reasons. In this case it is because they are a relatively small and privileged group, grossly over-represented in the state and parastatal bureaucracy and in commerce, with vested interests.

Although the contending groups have clear political and economic interests, the political process set in motion since the EPRDF victory of May 1991 has a life of its own. The past two years have seen an unprecedented public debate about the future of Ethiopia, inside and outside the country. The EPRDF's public commitment to democracy, human rights and national self-determination has also generated feverish discussion about these subjects. The political process has been removed from the exclusive control of the political organizations that initiated the dialogue. This was neither fully intended nor welcomed by the political organizations, including the EPRDF, but the consequence is that the political whole is more than the sum of its parts. This remains true despite the marked narrowing of the political space in late 1992.

The EPRDF

Despite its rhetoric that it is but one coalition partner in the Transitional Government, the EPRDF is both the brains and the muscle of the government. The EPRDF is, in large part, the Tigrayan People's Liberation Front (TPLF). About two-thirds of the EPRDF fighters are TPLF, and the same is true of the political leadership. Tigrayans represent no more than about 5 million of the total Ethiopian population of 50 million. The TPLF was founded in 1975 by a small group of radical students whose leadership has always been close knit and highly disciplined.[3] The present leaders emerged in 1985, which was a crucial year for the Front's development.

In 1985, the existence of not only the TPLF but the entire Tigrayan people appeared to be under threat from sustained military assault and man-made famine. It was Tigray's darkest hour. The secret of the EPRDF victory in 1991 lies in the TPLF's response to that year's seemingly impossible challenges when it launched a thorough review of its military, political, social and economic strategies. This resulted in the triumph of the Meles Zenawi's Marxist–Leninist League of Tigray (MLLT) and the demise of the former leadership of Berihu Aregawi and his followers. At root, Meles's strategy was extremely simple. It was to link the economic survival of the peasantry to the political and military fortunes of the TPLF. Every peasant in Tigray was aware that the Dergue was creating famine; Meles ensured that they recognized that supporting the TPLF provided the only prospect for eliminating famine. In 1985 and the subsequent years, TPLF strategy was designed to assist famine survival strategies in every possible way, including the adoption of pragmatic free market economic principles. This was a resounding success.

The other pillar of the TPLF's success was the system of elected village assemblies, known as *baitos*. These gave Tigrayan peasants an unprecedented democratic control over local affairs. The *baito* system has been widely admired for its success in promoting land redistribution, environmental protection schemes and social reforms such as women's rights, and for its efficiency in distributing famine relief. Though derived from models in the Leninist literature, it is essentially an indigenous creation.

The TPLF's mobilization of the Tigrayan peasantry was assisted by the relatively simple social formations in the region. The aristocracy having been removed by the 1974 revolution, a relatively homogeneous peasantry existed, further unified by a common experience of terror, war and famine under the Dergue.

The TPLF also played upon the Tigrayans' long-standing nationalism, and, more generally, on the antipathy of the northern Amhara to the Shewan Amhara who were seen as ruling the country (see below). From the start, national and ethnic consciousness was a central plank in the TPLF programme. This was articulated as the need for the liberation of subjugated and oppressed nationalities in Ethiopia.

In 1981 the TPLF brought under its wing a breakaway faction of the Ethiopian People's Revolutionary Party (EPRP), the Ethiopian People's Democratic Movement (EPDM). The TPLF had fought the EPRP in 1977 and was to do so on several occasions over the following decade. Despite its origins as a multiethnic pan-Ethiopian organization, the EPDM was to become the "Amhara wing" of the EPRDF. Until the mid-1980s, the TPLF made common cause with the OLF, to the extent of providing military assistance to OLF operations in areas where the government had forcibly resettled Tigrayan peasants. However, after 1986 a rift developed over the OLF's continuing support for an independent Oromia. In 1989 the TPLF founded the Oromo People's Democratic Organization (OPDO) as a rival to the OLF. Its ranks were formed chiefly by prisoners of war who agreed to fight against the Dergue. At the same time, the EPRDF was founded as an umbrella for the three groups.

Since the May 1991 victory, EPRDF ranks have been expanded as people in central and southern Ethiopia have joined. These people, who have mainly joined the EPDM and OPDO, did not participate in the armed struggle. The new recruits are vetted, but this has inevitably diluted the identity of the core organization. The influence of the new membership on EPRDF policies remains to be seen.

The TPLF-/EPRDF has displayed enormous organizational talents and a tremendous capacity for discipline. Its fighters are renowned for their disciplined behaviour, reflecting a combination of traditional Tigrayan values and the ideology of the Front.

Throughout the war, the leadership of the TPLF-/EPRDF was isolated, both intellectually and geographically, from the rest of the world. This has contributed to their somewhat eclectic ideology, and the fact that they are often patronized and despised by many of their peers who remained in Addis Ababa or fled abroad. In return, the leadership is secretive, and intolerant of outside criticism.

Its isolation also led the leadership to develop an extraordinarily profound understanding of the functioning of rural Tigrayan society, because they spent their years in the field talking to peasants, not to politicians. As discussed above, this was the key to the TPLF's success. One of the problems facing the current leadership is that this understanding does not easily transfer to other areas of the country.

One of the central questions relating to the EPRDF is the extent to which it still adheres to a Marxist–Leninist ideology. One answer is that the most recent EPRDF congress, in early 1991 (before the May victory), remained formally Marxist–Leninist. As there has been no subsequent congress, the position remains unchanged.

In part, the EPRDF's Marxism-Leninism is simply an intellectual legacy of the leaders' radical student days in the 1970s, fostered by years of isolation. In part, it follows on from the success of textbook Leninist principles in mobilizing the Tigrayan peasantry in the 1980s. Marxist economic policies may have been dropped, but Leninist organization still plays an important rôle in EPRDF thinking and this is manifest in its organizational principles.

The EPRDF formulated a Leninist two-stage theory of the revolution. The first stage was national democratic revolution and the second stage, socialist revolution. Strategic alliance with various groups was permitted for the first stage, but not for the second. Between the two stages was a transition period which had to be managed so that the possibility of moving on to the second stage was not lost. This required denying democratic rights to certain reactionary forces and putting the required structural transformations of the country's political life in place so that "democratic forces" were allowed to have their way. In this context, "democracy" does not allow a plurality of parties, but rather a plurality of opinions within one overall objective. It is a pyramidal form of self-government, with villages, districts and provinces each regulating their own affairs, and central policy being dictated by the considered outcome of all these local deliberations. This pyramidal structure is reflected both in the *baito* system of Tigray and in the June 1992 regional elections.

In this Leninist sense, the "transition period" takes on a quite different hue from that implied by the liberal language of the July 1991 Charter. Control of the transition is the key to the fulfilment of the EPRDF's programme.

If the EPRDF remains true to its Leninist principles, having won its hard-fought victory, it will remain determined to create a democracy in its own image. It will not be prepared to hand over its victory to the forces it sees as bourgeois and reactionary, whose notion of democracy is predicated on continued control of the state by urban elites. This was expressed in Resolutions 1 and 2 of the first EPRDF Congress of January 1991. These stressed the organization of "popular assemblies", rather than "occasions on which the masses 'elect' their oppressors every so often", and the denial of unrestricted democratic rights to "anti-popular and anti-democratic forces" (specifically, those who held power under either the Dergue or the Emperor). Neither would the EPRDF yield to organizations without a coherent political platform other than national independence or liberation (specifically the "independence wing" of the OLF). Resolution 3 of the EPRDF Congress granted nationalities the right to self-determination, including secession, but only after a full and fair referendum.

Having dealt separately with Eritrea, the congress also stated that, under conditions of democracy, secession would not "safeguard the interests of the people" – implicitly closing the door to secession in the case of a democratic government. The alternative answer to the question of Leninism is that the experience of government has so changed the EPRDF that its commitment to Leninism is merely a piece of historical baggage. Some of the creations of earlier years have been quietly abandoned – no more has been heard of the Revolutionary Ethiopian Workers' Party (created at the Second Congress), and the MLLT has adopted an extremely low profile. The new members of the EPRDF will undoubtedly dilute its former identity. Equally importantly, President Meles Zenawi and his immediate circle have displayed remarkable pragmatism.

Ultimately, the question of the EPRDF's commitment to Leninism must remain unresolved. The most probable answer is that in some respects, and to a limited degree, the EPRDF will continue to display Leninist principles of organization, but these will gradually be watered down by experience in government. However, hostility to "bourgeouis" notions of liberal democracy are likely to remain – not least because the EPRDF would not win any nationwide election held along Western multi-party lines.

Oromo groups

The Oromo are the largest people in Ethiopia, but remain politically fragmented. They have been traditionally marginalized in Ethiopian politics, "always on the outside looking in".[4] At the same time, successive governments have succeeded in co-opting significant sections of the Oromo.

Militant Oromo politics are centred around the OLF and several other fronts with similar agendas, notably the Islamic Front for the Liberation of Oromia (IFLO) and a group headed by the veteran rebel leader Wako Gutu. The OLF is itself splintered: it was founded in the east before being taken over by Christian westerners, and still shows the fault line. As a general rule, Oromos from Harerghe (east) agitate for independence, while those from Wollega (west) are prepared to accept a degree of autonomy within a united Ethiopia. Strong traditions of Oromo politics in the various Oromo regions have existed for centuries. It is only since the 1960s, and the creation of aspirations for a united independent Oromia, that pan-Oromo movements have been attempted.

The predicament of the OLF can be illustrated by a comparison of its fate with that of the TPLF in the mid-1980s. In 1982–3, there can be no doubt that the OLF presented a more formidable threat to the Dergue than the TPLF: it controlled most of the eastern highlands. However, while the war and famine of 1983–5 strengthened the TPLF, it all but destroyed the OLF. The OLF was unable to build a strong united leadership, and was unable to move beyond shallow nationalist politics towards a deeper articulation of the needs of the Oromo peasantry. In part, this was because of the high degree of class, regional and religious differentiation among the Oromo, and also the continued existence of powerful traditional elites. This meant that the OLF remained a more pluralistic and diffuse organization than the TPLF, with many different loci of power and authority, and differing local forms of organization. While this was democratic, it also meant that building an effective military machine was almost impossible. In addition, the organization was unable to build upon the concrete experiences of Oromo peasants to build a political programme. The OLF programme still consists largely of platitudes about democracy and human rights, and a general commitment to self-determination for the Oromo people.

An important element in the OLF political programme is psychology. Many Oromos have a strong tendency to regard themselves as victims, and remain more at ease in politically peripheral positions than in governmental office. They have a deep ambivalence towards the state, and a distrust of almost any manifestation of state power. Self-deprecation and deliberate half-heartedness about participation in government have led the Oromo to miss important political opportunities – and, having missed them, their leaders reassure themselves that their scepticism was warranted, as events have not developed to their liking.

In part, this scepticism is rooted in the recent historical experience of the 1974 revolution. The revolution was seen by the former ruling classes as, first, an Eritrean revolution and, secondly, an Oromo revolution. "National self-determination" was one of the slogans of the revolution during 1974–6, with reference primarily to Eritrea but also with powerful resonances in the south. The Dergue launched a literacy campaign using many vernacular languages, and ended the official use of the derogatory term "Galla". As David and Marina Ottoway noted, "These measures greatly encouraged the revival of ethnic feelings among all groups, particularly Gallas . . . There was no doubt that some top Dergue leaders deliberately encouraged the resurgence of ethnic consciousness. Chief among these was Major Mengistu himself."[5] Many Oromo leaders joined the revolution, notably Haile Fida of "Meison" (the All-Ethiopia Socialist Movement). They were rewarded with the chance to implement measures such as the land reform proclamation of 1975. However, by mid-1978 the Dergue turned against Meison, and bloodily purged it. It also undermined the progressive reforms of the early years of the revolution. The disastrous result of this compromise with the Dergue has coloured Oromo politicians' attitudes towards reformist central governments ever since.

The fragmented organization of the OLF has meant that, since May 1991, there has been a scramble for the allegiance of the Oromo. The OPDO has played the classic rôle of trying to co-opt a significant section of the Oromo people, with some success in the more centralist-oriented regions. In the east, the OLF and IFLO have vied for more radical positions, effectively undermining the negotiations for regional autonomy, elections and encampment of forces taking place in Addis Ababa. The OLF recruited more troops to its army, repeatedly attacked EPRDF military positions and destroyed more bridges in the year after the fall of Mengistu than in the 17 years of his rule. This, in turn, has given ample excuses for the EPRDF forces to refuse to encamp, and to engage in military actions against the OLF.

"Amhara" centralists

Who are the Amharas? This question has been at the heart of much historical, anthropological and political writing on Ethiopia. Several groups can be identified. One is the large majority of the peasants of the northern regions of Gojjam, Gondar, much of highland Wollo and northern Shewa. These people speak the Amharic language and have a cluster of common cultural traits, such as adherence to Orthodox Christianity, certain traditions of land tenure and social organization and the use of certain agricultural technologies such as ox ploughs. Another group is the "neftnennya", settlers in the southern regions who were closely associated with the Empire's landowning, governing and military classes. A third category is the urbanized or government-related ruling class. Historically, these people have formed the core of an indigenous conquest state, and have social attitudes to match. Many were assimilated from other ethnic groups and have "become Amhara" by adopting the Amharic language, Orthodox Christianity and other cultural traits. These latter two categories formed the bulk of the army's officer class and the governmental bureaucracy.[6]

The former ruling class has been described as "Shewan", because it is from there that most of its members originate. The Shewans came to dominance with the Emperor Menelik in the 1880s. Both Menelik's and Haile Selassie's governments were in the paradoxical position of being regarded as "Amhara" by the southerners and "Galla" by the northerners. The northerners, including the inhabitants of the traditional Abyssinian polity of Gojjam, Gondar and highland Wollo, regarded the Shewan ruling class as an assimilated group without authentic Amhara lineages.[7] However, the opposition of the northern Amhara was quelled through a deft mixture of military force, diplomacy and the use of a northern-based political symbolism. In the mid-1970s, Mengistu took many draconian actions against the Shewan elite, but after the military crises of 1977 the middle ranks of the former ruling class were able to re-establish their influence over the government.

Perhaps the most accurate description of the former ruling class is "centralist". This is because the Shewan core incorporated large numbers of Oromos, Tigrayans, Gurages and others who had assimilated to its values. (This does not negate the value of either the "Amhara" or "Shewan" labels.) The term "centralist" will be used here.

The centralists are politically fragmented, ranging from conservatives who are prepared to co-operate pragmatically with the Transitional Government to the remnants of the EPRP, which violently opposes it, and even includes some professed admirers of Mengistu. Though there is no explicitly formulated core programme, the centralists' main aim is to retain their privileged position in the army, bureaucracy and commerce. At present, their position in the first is destroyed, in the second is under threat and in the third remains unchallenged.

This set of objectives is often wrapped in a set of political beliefs that are best termed "Abyssinian fundamentalism". Its adherents are characterized by a psychological identification with a "Greater Ethiopia" (especially pronounced among exiles) and a belief in the superiority of the values of Ethiopian centralism over all other values found within the borders of the country (and beyond), with the consequence that the adherents to these values have a right to rule. For most, opposition to Eritrean independence is absolute. The political symbolism of the pre-revolutionary period plays an important part in these beliefs, which have a combination of naïvety and fervour such that they truly warrant the description "fundamentalism". Despite its anachronistic nature, Abyssinian fundamentalism is a cultural–political phenomenon with deep roots in Ethiopia, which will not be eradicated by an adverse turn of events, such as the EPRDF victory.

The centralist groups lack coherent organization and leadership. Some are determined to resort to force to remove the present government, while others prefer to play by the rules that it has created, convinced that ruling the country will be impossible without their support, so that they can ultimately co-opt the EPRDF's agenda.

Despite their essentially anachronistic and necessarily confrontational political agenda, and their lack of organization in opposition, the centralists hold another enormously important political card: bureaucratic competence. Until 1991 the ideological coherence and perceived common interest of the centralists provided Ethiopia with a central government that exercised more real power throughout the country than almost any other in sub-Saharan Africa. Just as Mengistu was compelled to turn to the professional army to rescue his regime in 1977, many centralists count on the fact that disorder in the south and economic chaos will compel the EPRDF to turn to the bureaucracy, and even to the reinstatement of former army officers. Such a reconciliation would cement any estrangement with the OLF and lead to the indefinite postponement of any plans for radical regionalization. This rapprochement would be more likely to occur through mutual assimilation than through a dramatic volte-face by the EPRDF leadership. The centralists' one necessary concession would be the independence of Eritrea, though many still harbour the fantasy that in a free vote Eritreans would vote for unity with Ethiopia.

Other groups

There are other, smaller political groups contending for a share of power in Ethiopia. Most of these represent smaller ethnic groups, or very peripheral groups. They include the Afar, the Ethiopian Somalis, the Sidama, the Gurage, the Adere, the Nuer, the Anuak and numerous others. They have failed to form any coherent bloc, on the whole being swayed by one or other of the three main power blocs, or strongly influenced by events in neighbouring countries.

Some peripheral groups hold key strategic positions, such as the Afar who straddle the road to Assab, and the Issa Somalis who control territory next to the railway line to Djibouti. States based in the highlands and dominated by Christian highlanders have traditionally failed to understand the nomadic societies on their borders, and have treated them with condescension as uncivilized people needing to be settled. However, over time, highland rulers have usually become adept at controlling lowland peoples through the manipulation of alliances and patronage, interspersed with the threat or use of military force. The TPLF-EPRDF has taken more than 15 years to begin to learn how to negotiate with the Afar, and is still not very good at it; its dealings with the ethnic Somalis are even less advanced. However, it will undoubtedly learn enough to keep Ethiopia's strategic peripheries relatively pacified.

The search for legitimacy

In the absence of democratic accountability, successful Ethiopian governments have been adept at manipulating political symbolism to obtain
domestic legitimacy and international recognition and support. This is both
a central element of the political process, and a disguise of the true nature
of that process. Ethiopian governments were, until 1991, unusual in Africa
in the power of their indigenous legitimating myths.

Emperor Haile Selassie used the Solomonic myth – his legendary descent
from King Solomon and the Queen of Sheba – combined with Orthodox
Christianity as his central legitimizing symbolism. This was founded on a
mythological history of three thousand years of unbroken independent
Ethiopian history. For the West and for certain domestic groups, he also
claimed to be a modernizer. His success in establishing his legitimacy
abroad was manifest in his restoration by British forces in 1941, and his
subsequent receipt of important military, economic and diplomatic support
from the West.

Colonel Mengistu Haile Mariam had a more difficult task in establishing
his legitimacy, precisely because he was the antithesis of the Emperor.
However, it is remarkable how far he succeeded. The popular attribution of
his ethnicity shows a trajectory from "Shankilla" (slave or ex-slave) in 1974
to Oromo and finally, by 1990, to his accreditation as a member of the
Amhara aristocracy, albeit born outside wedlock.[8] Mengistu skilfully used
several legitimizing myths. First he was a "social bandit" opposing the
hated aristocracy, then heroic nationalist opposing the Somali invader, then
conqueror whose might was right; later he used variants of all three deeply
rooted Ethiopian symbols. Mengistu also cultivated the myths about his
ancestry. His favourite historical comparison was the ruthless 19th-century
unifier of Ethiopia, Emperor Teodros, and, had he ruled longer, he would
probably have officially established a direct line of descent. Mengistu's communist rhetoric was aimed at certain elements of the educated classes and
the Soviet Union, from which it succeeded in eliciting massive military
assistance, including 1,400 tanks.

The EPRDF, in its original manifestation as the TPLF, successfully employed
Tigrayan nationalism and an ideology of liberation to defeat Mengistu. The
OLF used national liberation, achieving little military success.

Since May 1991, there has been a vacuum of pan-Ethiopian political symbolism, causing great anxiety among certain sections of the population, particularly the centralists. This is for two associated reasons. First, the EPRDF
is the antithesis of the Dergue and it is attempting an ambitious transformation of Ethiopia's entire political structure, including a rejection of all the
old centralist legitimizing symbols. Secondly, the EPRDF has generated a real
political process in Addis Ababa, rather than using simple authoritarian rule
disguised in legitimizing symbolism.

The political process had, in its early months at least, a genuine open-ness, despite its many flaws and the scepticism of large sections of the population. The concepts of democracy, human rights and national–ethnic self-determination have developed a life of their own.

The June 1991 regional elections were Ethiopia's first major exercise in democracy in Ethiopia but they were badly flawed. In many areas there were no competitive elections to speak of, largely because the organization in military command of the area had ensured that genuine opposition can-didates were unable to stand. Both the EPRDF and the OLF were guilty of such intimidation. Voting procedures on the day were generally acceptable, and a handful of independent and opposition candidates were returned. Under pressure, the government set up a commission to investigate elector-al malpractices. The government and OLF still controlled the main media outlets, but independent critical publications were allowed. While not an exercise in Western-style multi-party democracy, neither were the elections wholly a Leninist hoax.

On human rights, the Transitional Government has a mixed record.[9] There have been marked improvements compared with the Mengistu Gov-ernment, but arbitrary detention still continues, and the legal system has yet to start functioning properly. The government has, however, committed itself to the principles of an independent judiciary and basic legal norms such as *habeus corpus*, and is prepared to admit to shortcomings in its programme. As the EPRDF has remained in power, however, its authoritar-ian instincts appear to have reasserted themselves more strongly. Mean-while, dissenters and political opponents have been using the issue of human rights as a campaigning platform.

Given the political coalition stitched together after the EPRDF victory, and the appalling record of successive centralist governments, the Transitional Government's commitment to some form of national self-determination was inevitable and necessary. This was reinforced by the need to find common ground with other ethnically based fronts, such as the Afar Liberation Front and various Somali groups. However, "self-determination" has taken on a life of its own. Both the EPRDF and OLF's ideas of what constitutes a "na-tionality" are pan-ethnic, based on common language, territorial contiguity and other factors. Many ethnic groups have interpreted self-determination as applying to any and all ethnic groups, and have laid claim to separate administrations and ethnically homogeneous territories. This is contributing to widespread unrest throughout southern Ethiopia which is seriously undermining confidence in the government. As elsewhere, ethnic identifica-tion has proved easy to initiate but difficult to contain. It is serving to erode the legitimacy of central government, ironically, amongst both the suppor-ters of political ethnicity and its detractors.

The whole political process in Addis Ababa is messy and confusing, but has at times demonstrated more popular accountability than at any other time in Ethiopian history. However, as opposition to the EPRDF's rule intensifies, and the government deals increasingly harshly with dissent, the window of democratic opportunity appears to be closing.

There is one country-level legitimizing symbolism open to the EPRDF: the right of conquest following its absolute defeat of Mengistu. The EPRDF's opponents have tried, unsuccessfully, to undermine this by constructing a myth that the EPRDF did not "win" but entered Addis Ababa only because of US perfidy and the refusal of Mengistu's army to fight. This is an historical absurdity but it provides a revealing insight into Ethiopian political symbolism, in which military might figures large. As its democratic credentials fade, the EPRDF will make the May 1991 victory more important in Ethiopian political culture in order to gain legitimacy.

This vacuum of legitimizing symbolism is also felt acutely in the West. Western nations have alternately idealized and demonized Ethiopian governments. In May 1991, they idealized the EPRDF's promise of "democracy". Those high hopes have now faded because there was no rapid creation of peace, stability, justice and democracy. In retrospect, the expectations were wholly unrealistic.

As the West's Ethiopian dream again unravels, there is no longer an obvious Western-based model for interpreting Ethiopia. It is no longer a Christian empire, nor a Marxist totalitarian state. The shrill condemnations of some exiled groups mainly reveal their political immaturity. The EPRDF is not a second Dergue; neither is it a tool of the Eritreans for dismembering once proud Ethiopia with the intent of creating anarchy, Somalia style. Demonization of the EPRDF is not an option. Western analysts are lost in the Ethiopia of 1993. Journalists can no longer fall back upon a well established shorthand to characterize the country, and any attempt to provide even the barest outlines of analysis exceeds the word limit permitted by most editors. A new set of paradigms is needed, which includes the recognition that the political symbolism used to interpret Ethiopia in the past was in fact founded more on obscurantist myth than on social or economic reality.

The economic basis of the state

Ethiopia today is a highly politicized country. Educated Ethiopians and resident foreigners are preoccupied with a narrow set of concerns related to the political process, to the exclusion of all else. The Transitional Government has devoted almost all its energies to issues such as regionalization, elections, ethnic self-determination and a series of agreements with the OLF, neglecting the disastrous economic situation. However, any understanding of the present problems in Ethiopia and their future direction must be based on the economy.

The Ethiopian state has never been built on the principle of wealth creation. Instead, it has always sustained itself through wealth extraction by forcibly controlling land, labour and assets of rural people, particularly in the south, and by extracting commodities at rates well below what would be established in a free market. Historically, the state was compelled to expand geographically, incorporating and subjugating new peripheries in order to generate new flows of wealth to the centre. After territorial expansion became impossible, the state instead created artificial frontiers (for instance by the resettlement programme) or turned to intensified exploitation of already incorporated areas (through villagization, the Agricultural Marketing Corporation (AMC) and tight regulation of trade). Under the Dergue, the process of expansion and extraction became self-defeating and has now been halted and even reversed.

Until the 1974 revolution, the state financed itself essentially from two sources. One was taxation on trade, and the other the extraction of "surplus" agricultural production predominantly from southern Ethiopian peasant farmers. This was facilitated by the land tenure system which gave a vast array of rights to landowners to appropriate much of their tenants' crops. That which was taken was not necessarily surplus to the tenant family's needs, and rural hunger was widespread. The Emperor reserved the power of granting land to his followers, who then lived off the labour of the inhabitants, and, in turn, the produce extracted was traded to supply the cities.

The revolution was a complex event, sparked by discontent in the army and among certain urban groups such as students, trade unionists and taxi drivers. There was war in Eritrea. In the southern rural areas, there was a widespread spontaneous insurrection against the landlords and the government (the two being correctly perceived as equal representatives of the state). The fragile Dergue was thus faced with a dilemma. Its political survival depended on recognizing the *fait accompli* of the southern uprisings; this it did by an act of great political imagination. The Dergue granted powers to local peasant associations (PA), and by doing so proclaimed a radical land reform that wholly abolished tenancy. This brought immediate economic benefit to the peasants and gave the Dergue immense political capital or legitimacy, especially in the Oromo areas. It thereby provided the breathing space to fight off four political–military threats: the feudal landowners, the radical students, the Somali invaders and the Eritrean fronts. It also helped defuse the threat posed by the newly formed OLF.

However, in recognizing the southern uprising, the Dergue had undermined the economic viability of the state. While southern peasants ate better than ever before, there were serious urban food shortages and worries about a possible fiscal crisis. Agricultural and economic policy in the 12 years following the land reform proclamation can be seen as a series of attempts to claw back control over the agricultural production of the south.

Thus, the PA leadership was purged and instead became an instrument of central rule; state farms were set up using forcibly recruited labour; the Agricultural Marketing Association the (AMC) was established, and delivery quotas for all crops were set for each PA; trading licences were revoked in an attempt to create a state monopoly on trade; northern populations were resettled on to state-run agricultural schemes; and finally, villagization of the entire rural population was attempted as a prelude to collectivization. These moves amounted to feudalism revisited under a socialist guise. The measures all had adverse effects for the southern peasants, whose gains in standard of living of the 1975-7 period were eroded, but it allowed the government to feed the army and the towns, and to finance itself. This also meant that the Dergue used up its political capital won in 1975, and by the time villagization was implemented, the Dergue was as hated in the south as in the north.

In the late 1980s, the government began the slow process of reversing some of its most disastrous economic policies. The snail's pace *perestroika* started with the liberalization of coffee prices in 1987, and culminated in the official abandonment of Marxist economic policies in March 1990. Had these reforms been given time, they would undoubtedly have strengthened the national economy and the fiscal foundations of the government. However, they were too late, too half-hearted, and were overtaken by political and military events, and thus served only to weaken the state. This was particularly true of the March 1990 liberalization, which was correctly interpreted by southern peasants as a sign of Mengistu's weakness rathern than his enlightenment. Farmers took the opportunity to seize control of their localities and to reverse the villagization programme by expelling cadres and government officers. As the Mengistu regime weakened still further and then fell, the government's control of the south slackened, so that by the time the EPRDF penetrated south from Addis Ababa, much of the south was effectively unadministered. It has remained so.

As in 1975, the Transitional Government was faced with the *fait accompli* of a fragmented, lawless south. Like the Dergue, the Transitional Government decided to address the political priorities before the economic ones, inviting the OLF into government and pushing ahead with regionalization. However, while the 1975 land reform brought immediate benefits (economic for the Oromo peasants, political for the state), these recent initiatives have so far yielded neither.

In other respects, the situation is radically changed from 1975. There are three major reasons for this. One is that the experience since 1975 has made the Ethiopian people extremely sceptical and unwilling to become politically engaged.

Second is the growth of external dependency in the 1980s. During the 17 years of the Dergue's rule, foreign aid to Ethiopia grew tenfold to top $1 billion (about 20 per cent of the gross national product). Most of this growth came in the mid and late 1980s. Foreign assistance has become an important source of tax revenue, foreign exchange and staple food. However, most of this aid is food, and per capita assistance levels remain very low by world standards.

The third reason is the decline in the capacity of the state to act and the current crisis of governance. Historically, Ethiopia has alternated between periods in which the central power was dominant and periods in which the regions were more powerful. The centralization of the late 19th century was undone in the first third of this century, despite the imperial trappings of the monarchy. As Margery Perham commented, "An official British report of 1906 states that [Emperor] Menelik is an absolute despot and a few paragraphs later remarks that his power does not extend twenty miles beyond his palace."[10] From the 1930s to 1991, with a brief interruption in 1975, the tendency has been centralist. While this uncompromising centralism has been probably the main reason behind the wars of the past three decades, it also contributed to the development of an effective governmental bureaucracy, informed by a coherent set of values and obedient to the wishes of central government, whether imperial or communist. Throughout the 1980s, Mengistu was able to implement titanic programmes of social engineering that other African governments could only dream of by using this bureaucracy. Western donors could prescribe policy reforms, confident that, if the political will to implement them was there, the machinery could be trusted to function accordingly.

There are a number of factors contributing to the recent decline in the functioning of the state. One is that the state is bankrupt. Haile Selassie followed an extremely cautious monetary policy and endowed his successors with large gold and foreign exchange reserves, and one of the most stable currencies in Africa. Despite its socialist policies, the Mengistu government followed the same fiscal conservatism.[11] However, no amount of adept central management could square the circle of massive military expenditure and declining tax revenues. Then came the most devastating blow: the collapse of world coffee prices in 1989. By 1991 the coffers were entirely empty. Civil service salaries were due three days after the EPRDF entered Addis Ababa and there was literally no money in the bank to pay.

A second factor is the mutual antipathy between the EPRDF and the bureaucracy. As discussed, the bureaucracy is a special, privileged class in Ethiopia, with particular class and ethnic characteristics. The government sees the bureaucrats as manifestations of all it fought against, and hence is unwilling to trust them to implement its programmes. The bureaucracy, already distrustful of the EPRDF and other fronts, has been made more so by this distance between itself and its new rulers, and hence has failed to co-operate to anything like the full extent. This non-co-operation has been heightened by the fear that the government will make large cuts in the public sector payroll, and by the operations of government-established Grievance Hearing Committees in 1991-2, in which employees passed arbitrary judgements on those in their institutions whom they deemed to be guilty of misconduct under the former regime.

Leaving aside the political estrangement involved, the economic ramifications of this semi-paralysis of the government machinery is highly significant. First, the Transitional Government has failed to develop a detailed economic policy, and it must now be questionable whether it would be able to implement such a policy were it drawn up. (However, since the withdrawal of the OLF from government in June 1992, there are signs that managerial and technical matters are being dealt with more quickly and efficiently.) Secondly, the state is now in a period of contraction. This is leaving many regional and economic spaces that can be filled by other centres of wealth extraction, some based on military power.

Economic liberalization can only further weaken the power of the state to implement policy. Liberalization will mean a reduction in the number of state employees and a severe cut in the standard of living of those who remain. Large areas over which the government currently retains control will pass from its grasp, and greater economic power will pass to the regions and classes with actual or potential access to foreign currency, such as the coffee growing areas of Harerghe, and those who have relatives abroad remitting hard currency.

Linked to this is a third point, which is that the Transitional Government is attempting to carry out an extremely ambitious reorganization of the country, notably with its regionalization programme. This involves dismantling much of the centralized bureaucracy and replacing it with a new set of regional bureaucracies. This is bound to be a lengthy and difficult process, involving a very inefficient use of existing human resources.

The one area in which the state enjoys increasing power and privilege *vis à vis* its subjects is in foreign aid. This is likely to take on increasing importance in the Ethiopian government. As noted above, the northerners need control of the state for survival and much of the benefit they hope to tap into consists of foreign aid. The design and conditionality of aid programmes will therefore become a crucial element in the division of power and the prospects for government in Ethiopia. There are three important elements here. One is the question of whether the agreements are signed with central or regional government, which will be a key factor in determining the viablility of regional governments. The second is economic conditionality. The Ethiopian economy is structurally inflexible, owing to the lack of infrastructure and the preponderence of smallholder farmers, so that classic structural adjustment formulae may yield relatively few benefits. There are encouraging signs that the major donors recognize this. Finally, there is the issue of political conditionality, specifically "democracy" and human rights. Here, it is important to recognize the interdependence of democratic accountability and economic progress. It is unrealistic to expect instant democracy in Ethiopia, and far more profitable to try to tie economic assistance into a *process* of increasing democratization, both supporting it and being conditional on it.

Despite the weakening power of the state, it remains the chief accessible source of economic reward. Control of the state is therefore likely to remain the subject of intense and probably violent competition.

Militarization

The character of the economy and the nature of state interference will be further changed by the local conflicts that are almost certain to become an enduring aspect of Ethiopian life. The structure of conflict is an important subject. There are interrelated elements. One is the legacy of armaments, the training in their use and the proclivity to violence left by the Dergue. This is compounded by the demobilization of Mengistu's armed forces, numbering 500,000 soldiers, who are left without employment. A second is the resurgence of inter-ethnic conflict, mostly in the south. A third is the manipulation of ethnic and other conflict by political organizations. Fourthly, there is conflict driven by competition for resources, including land, water, livestock, trade routes (including check points), state benefits (such as rationed commodities), international aid or government office. The conflicts are essentially destructive, but once the cycle of violence and deprivation is set in motion, it is exceptionally difficult to break. The paradigm for this type of conflict is the turmoil in Somalia. However, this is extremely unlikely in Ethiopia, which retains sufficient traditional structures and central authority to prevent such chaos.

Much of the conflict in the southeast arises out of this combination of factors. This makes it difficult for the OLF to create an effective centralized guerrilla army that would be a serious threat to the government. Conversely, it also makes it difficult for the government to defeat any insurgency using conventional methods of military action and control of the population. The model for counter-insurgency strategies in the south is likely to be closer to the doctrine of the "oil spot" spreading over unadministered territory, employed by the French in Morocco at the beginning of this century.

Unfortunately for the central government, these local conflicts are occurring in economically vital parts of the country (notably Harerghe) and, for that reason alone, cannot be dealt with at leisure. By contrast, Tigray and rural Eritrea contributed very little to the national economy, so the wars there had a much smaller economic impact.

Conclusion

How is a Western analyst to find his or her way in contemporary Ethiopia? Some detachment and historical perspective are necessary, to avoid the feverish optimism and pessimism characteristic of those who are too closely involved with the political process. Currently, no readily available paradigm fits, so we must be content with a fair degree of confusion.

Prediction is hazardous. Just as almost every pre–1974 prediction for the future of Ethiopia proved hopelessly inaccurate as the revolution unfolded, so almost every prognosis made before Mengistu fell has failed to describe the events since he was defeated.

More important, is the question of how the Transitional Government is to find its way. The key lies in the recognition of two facts. One is that, while a radical transformation of the political structure of Ethiopia is undoubtedly necessary, current circumstances are extremely inauspicious. The "stubborn, enduring strength" that is the most valued quality of the Tigrayan peasant,[12] which the EPRDF has already amply demonstrated in its war against Mengistu, will be called upon again, together with other skills of diplomacy and tolerance.

Patience is therefore needed. A two-year transitional period is almost certainly too short. The experience of the first year demonstrated that multi-party politicking would consume the energies of the government, to the neglect of other institutions and concerns equally central to the establishment of a democratic civil society, such as the judiciary, the police and army, the press and, of course, the economy. The experience of the second year appeared to show that, stripped of the constraints of an effective legal opposition, the EPRDF was reverting to authoritarian intolerance. The problems of multi-partyism are not an argument for aborting the pluralist political process, rather one for ensuring that other safeguards and structures of accountability are also developed.

The second fact is that the success of the Transitional Government depends on its being able to deliver tangible economic benefits to the people, rapidly. The two most successful political initiatives in modern Ethiopia – by the Dergue in 1975 and the TPLF in 1985 – were based upon articulating rural Ethiopian's basic material needs with certain political programmes. A similar linkage is needed now. Unfortunately, economic liberalization will not provide it; the only immediate alternative is large-scale foreign aid. This is the immediate challenge for Ethiopia's donors: to provide assistance in such a way that ordinary Ethiopians begin to have confidence in their future material security.

Acknowledgements

A previous version of this chapter appeared in *World Policy Journal* 9 (1992), 719–38.

Notes

1. "Evil days: thirty years of war and famine in Ethiopia", *Africa Watch* (1991),.
2. Ethiopian ethnic politics follows the Marxist terminology of "nationalities", made familiar by the breakup of the Soviet Union and Yugoslavia.
3. For an account of the TPLF see Gebru Tareke, "Preliminary history of peasant resistance in Tigrai (Ethiopia)", *Africa* 39 (1984), 213–14.
4. P. Baxter, "'Always on the outside looking in': a view of the 1969 Ethiopian elections from a rural constituency", *Ethnos* 1(2) (1980), 41–59.
5. M. Ottoway & D. Ottoway, *Ethiopia: empire in revolution*, p. 91 (New York: Africana, 1978).
6. C. Clapham, *Transformation and continuity in revolutionary Ethiopia* (Cambridge: Cambridge University Press, 1988).
7. G. Salole, "Who are the Shoans?" *Horn of Africa* 2 (1978), 20–9.
8. Rene Lefort, *Ethiopia: an heretical revolution?* (London: Zed Press, 1983).
9. "Ethiopia: waiting for justice: shortcomings in establishing the rule of law", News from *Africa Watch* (May 1992).
10. M. Perham, *The government of Ethiopia*, 2nd edn, p. 72 (London: Faber & Faber, 1969).
11. R. Love, "Funding the Ethiopia state: who pays?" *Review of African Political Economy* 44 (1989), 18–26.
12. K. E. Knutsson & R. Selinus, "Fasting in Ethiopia: an anthropological and nutritional study", *American Journal of Clinical Nutrition* 23 (1970), 956–67.

CHAPTER FOUR
Descent into chaos:
Somalia, January 1991 – December 1992

PATRICK GILKES

Siad Barre's last days in power were spent in a city that he had been large-ly responsible for turning into a battleground. It mirrored the country at large, and his legacy of clan feuding will take years to dissipate. He and his Marehan guard were driven out of Mogadishu by the Hawiye guerrillas of the United Somali Congress (USC), supported by a mass uprising sparked off by indiscriminate artillery bombardment of Hawiye areas of the city. After Siad fled, the Hawiye took revenge on members of his Marehan clan and on the Darod clan family to which the Marehan belong. (The other clans in the Darod are Majerteen, Ogaden, Dolbuhunta and Warsengeli.) Hundreds of Darod were killed and there were also allegations that as many Hawiye were killed by Siad Barre's fleeing troops.

Siad Barre fled from Mogadishu as his enemies closed in on his resi-dence, the "Villa Somalia", on 27 January 1991. He took refuge in his home area in the northwest after making one final effort to divide his opponents by announcing a new government on 20 January and by offering to give up power in exchange for a cease fire. It had no effect. By then there was nothing left. The army was in total disarray and numbered only a few thousand. By the end of the 1980s the command structure had collapsed, largely as a result of the over-swift promotion of untrained Marehan. A considerable number of people who had been lieutenants in 1978 had been promoted to colonels or even generals by 1990. The collapse was paralleled in the bureaucracy and the administration, and by 1990, with many of its institutions having been in decay for years, Somalia had effectively ceased to exist as a state.

The USC announced its takeover on 29 January 1991, and invited all opposition groups to participate in a national conference. Two days later, however, it announced that Ali Mahdi Mohammed, a former politician in pre–1969 governments and more recently a wealthy businessman and hotel owner, had been appointed acting president. There was immediate con-demnation from other clans despite USC protestations that it did not mean to form a permanent government. It pointed to its efforts to incorporate other leading figures. A prominent Isaaq and one-time foreign minister, Omar Arteh, was appointed prime minister, but he was seen as having been compromised by his acceptance of the premiership on 20 January just before Siad fell. The two main opposition groups to Siad, the Somali Salvation Democratic Front (SSDF) and the Somali National Movement (SNM), both found him unacceptable. More important was the appointment of General Mohammed Abshir, the head of police before 1969 and for many years a detainee under Siad Barre. Within a few weeks, however, he went into Majerteen clan territory in the northeast, to help try and solve the difficulties between the USC and SSDF in the central regions. He did not return to the government of Ali Mahdi.

The majority of posts in the new government were filled by Hawiye, who had been involved in the series of manifestos critical of government policy, the so-called Manifesto Group. The manifestos began to appear in 1990, and all of the guerrilla groups felt that this was rather late to have come to the struggle against Siad Barre's regime.

The USC were taken aback by the criticisms. Ali Mahdi and the Manifesto Group had expected nothing but praise for their expulsion of Siad Barre from Mogadishu, but the negative response to what they continued to insist was a temporary government forced them to agree to a reconciliation conference sponsored by President Hassan Gouled in Djibouti. At the first meeting the USC was joined by the Somali Democratic Movement (SDM – a Rahenwein organization, operating to the immediate north and west of Mogadishu), the Somali Salvation Democratic Front (SSDF) (Majerteen) and the Somali Patriotic Movement (SPM) (Ogaden). At the second meeting these were joined by the Somali Democratic Alliance (SDA) (Gadabursi) and the United Somali Front (USF) (Issa). However, the Issaq-dominated Somali National Movement (SNM) had declared the independence of the north in May, a move supported by the elders of all the northern clans including both the Gadabursi and the Issa.

The Djibouti meetings did not provide much in the way of reconciliation. An agreement was hammered out committing the participants to wage all-out war on Siad Barre, implement a general ceasefire, respect national unity, readopt the 1960 constitution and allow Ali Mahdi two years as interim president. A great deal of the discussion related to the division of ministerial appointments. The Darod groups (SSDF and SPM) pushed hard for a Darod prime minister; others wanted a northerner, and not Omar Arteh, who came in for a lot of criticism; in fact, the SSDF said that his removal was one of their criteria for accepting the final communiqué.

Another point raised by the Darod groups was for Darod property, seized in the aftermath of Siad Barre's flight, to be returned. This remained a matter of serious contention. It has been estimated that the Darod and Isaaq between them owned as much as 60 per cent of the houses in Mogadishu before 1989, while making up no more than 40 per cent of the population). Most of this property was looted after Siad Barre's flight and many of the houses taken over, in the absence of their previous owners, by Hawiye. They will be difficult to dislodge even if the claimants do reappear. As national unity conferences, the Djibouti meetings were stillborn, although the agreement was subsequently used by Ali Mahdi as legitimizing a two-year term of office for himself as president in the disputes that arose within the USC with General Aydeed, who was elected chairman of the USC in the middle of the year.

A major factor in the difficulties of Ali Mahdi and the Manifesto Group has been the split within the USC and the Hawiye. The USC was formed when some Hawiye elements in the SNM left the organization in the late 1980s and set up the USC in Rome in 1989. Other elements, notably from the Habr Gidir, one of the main divisions of the Hawiye, and particularly from the Saad and Salaban subclans, set up an alternative version of the USC under General Mohammed Farah "Aydeed" to carry out military operations in central Somalia. The Habr Gidir, which have five subgroups, make up most of the rural elements of the Hawiye. The other main Hawiye subclan is the Abgal, which has nine divisions and makes up much of the population in and around Mogadishu. In May 1990, when the Manifesto Group first surfaced publicly in Mogadishu, it brought together people from several different clans; but the driving force was the Abgal, who wanted to organize their own guerrilla forces under the USC label. This was in part to pre-empt and control Hawiye groups already taking up arms in the countryside near Mogadishu and to ensure Abgal leadership in any Hawiye organization. Those involved included Ali Mahdi, who provided much of the finance; Hassan Haji Mohammed "Bod", an ex-parliamentarian and chairman of the USC executive committee who surfaced after Siad fled; and Ahmed Mohammed Darman, a former ambassador to Iran.

The arrival of General Aydeed in Mogadishu with his USC guerrillas from non-Abgal subclans, including the Saad, Ayr and Salaban (Habr Gidir), rapidly provoked a crisis. The Saad, in particular, have contempt for the "soft living" city dwellers and feel the Abgal have betrayed their nomadic origins. There was resentment of the wealth of the city and of what they saw as the government's failure to provide adequate rewards for *mudjadeen* fighters. It was particularly galling that Ali Mahdi himself and others were seen as having grown rich during Siad's time in power. General Aydeed and his men bitterly resented the way in which they felt Ali Mahdi and the Manifesto politicians had seized power for themselves while the guerrillas had fought to bring Siad down. Indeed, General Aydeed himself appears to have taken this personally, making it immediately clear that he felt that Ali Mahdi had no right to assume the presidency, whether acting or not. In July 1991 Aydeed was elected chairman of the USC and achieved a power base within the organization. From then on it was merely a matter of time before the relationship between the two men exploded into violence. Ali Mahdi's failure to provide any government posts to Aydeed's supporters in an August 1991 government reshuffle after the Djibouti conference provided an easy excuse.

The first clash came in September 1991, when four days of fighting left hundreds dead and thousands wounded. This was just a mild preview of the serious hostilities which broke out in November and lasted until 3 March 1992 when a ceasefire held – more or less. Half a dozen previous attempts to obtain a ceasefire agreement had failed within hours. The March 1992 agreement held because both sides were exhausted, ammunition was running low and food supplies were desperately short, with no international body prepared or indeed able to intervene until the fighting stopped. By then at least 30,000 had died and thousands more had been injured. The city was almost torn apart.

In the first months there was no shortage of material to fight with. All the police, military and security armouries had been emptied in the fight to oust Siad Barre. Prices in the Kaaran gun markets fell to $50 for an AK47 (with ammunition about 12 cents a bullet), $100 for an RPG7 in good condition and $200 for a bazooka. Substantial areas had been depopulated as soon as, or shortly after, Siad Barre fled in January 1991 when the Darod and particularly the Marehan felt threatened enough to follow suit. The later fighting led to other population movements, with hundreds of thousands fleeing the city to try to escape the fighting. The remaining Isaaq and other northerners who had stayed finally abandoned their houses to the Hawiye.

The struggle had been complicated by the presence in Mogadishu of two other Hawiye clan militias – the Hawadle and the Murasade. Both were ostensibly neutral, but the Hawadle, holding the airport, favoured General Aydeed while the Murasade, holding the port, backed Ali Mahdi. The ceasefire was organized by the UN Special Envoy, James Jonah. It enabled some food supplies to be brought in, but the failure to co-opt other Hawiye clans allowed the Murasade to show their displeasure by firing on the first UN ship trying to dock, eventually forcing it off. Subsequently arrangements were made to hire fighters as guards, and by May 1991 food was beginning to arrive in some quantity. The UN then came in for a lot of criticism for making too little effort to achieve a wider solution to Somalia's problems, although there were various mediation efforts by the OAU and the Arab League, as well as by individual states, in the first few months of 1992.

The conflict in Mogadishu became a personalized fight between Aydeed and Ali Mahdi fuelled by the rivalry between the Habr Gidir and the Abgal as a whole. But by early March 1992 support for both men was weakening as neither appeared capable of winning. Ali Mahdi could count on the Harti and several other Abgal subclans, but even some of these were beginning to question his leadership, and his Murasade allies were restless. He still, however, maintained a larger, if less well armed, force than Aydeed whose Habr Gidir were also showing signs of exhaustion. Most of the Saad and the Salabaan had come to Mogadishu with Aydeed in 1991, and the Habr Gidir had few reserves left; their manpower was literally running out. As a result, both General Aydeed and Ali Mahdi tried to raise allies elsewhere. Ali Mahdi looked to the groups that attended the Djibouti conference which he regarded as having legitimized his position as president. Most of his ministers went abroad, several attempting to drum up support in the Arab League or the UN. They had little success, and Ali Mahdi failed to get the full international recognition he wanted and needed.

Ali Mahdi's main effort to acquire allies was directed to the SSDF, though he had little success until the latter part of 1992 after General Aydeed's victories in the south made him look more threatening. By mid-1991 the SSDF was running its own administration in the Majerteen northeastern area. General Mohammed Abshir was chosen as SSDF chairman at a executive committee meeting in May 1992, and the former SSDF leader, Colonel Abdullahi Yusuf, became deputy chairman, though the relationship between the two men was uneasy. Colonel Abdullahi criticized General Abshir for having too close a connection with Ali Mahdi; he himself had close links with General Aydeed – they trained together in Italy and were in imprisoned together for several years by Siad Barre.

Colonel Abdullahi was also reported to regard General Abshir as being too close to Islam. This had considerable significance after Islam emerged as a serious political force for the first time in June 1992. An uprising by the Islamic party, al-Itahad, seized several towns including Garowe and Bosasso. A large number of SSDF leaders were captured, including both General Abshir and Colonel Abdullahi, but released. Popular resistance forced al-Itahad out of all but Bosasso where they had been closely involved in relief operations. As a non-clan grouping they had been widely trusted by Bosasso's local people, though relations with the SSDF had deteriorated in the previous few months with allegations that al-Itahad had been using port profits to build up arms supplies. The uprising had apparently been timed to coincide with a concentration of SSDF forces further south facing the Hawiye. Once released, Colonel Abdullahi Yusuf hurriedly brought SSDF forces back to besiege Bosasso. When the the al-Itahad commander, Colonel Abdulrashid Guled Warfa, was killed, Bosasso was retaken on 28 June 1992. The remnants of the al-Itahad fled west into Somaliland, into Warsengeli areas, to the port of Las Khorey, which they were still holding in early 1993. They appeared to have some support in the north – the distribution of leaflets attacking relief operations and warning international agencies to leave in Hargeisa early in 1993 was thought to be their work.

The al-Itahad also had considerable strength in other southern towns, including Merca and Lugh. An Islamic congress was held in Merca in mid-

August 1992, and reports spoke of Iranian and Sudanese delegations being present. In November 1992 General Aydeed spoke of the need for Somalia to be ruled in accordance with Shari'a law, suggesting he had some concern about Islamic groups in the areas he controlled, including Merca. The Islamic "threat", although apparently small and localized, was taken seriously by both Kenya and the United States. The anarchic situation in Somalia was seen as a "breeding ground for the virus of fundamentalism". The United States was particularly concerned by what it saw as the spreading influence of the Iran–Sudan connection and its links into Ethiopia, Eritrea and parts of Somalia. Such a view might have been extreme, but it appears to have been one reason behind the US intervention in December 1992.

To begin with, General Aydeed did better in organizing a coalition. He had close relations with the Southern Somali National Movement (SSNM), led by Abdi Warsame Isaaq, an organization of non-Darod largely from the Kismayo area. The SSNM regards itself as the southern branch of the SNM. He also made an alliance with one of the three factions of the SDM (Rahenwein). One faction was associated with Ali Mahdi's first vice-president Abdulkadir Mohammed Adan ("Soobe"); the second, Abdi Selaam Sheikh Hussein, a former minister of higher education, lined up alongside the Somali National Front (SNF); the third, under Mohammed Nur Aliyon, allied with General Aydeed.

General Aydeed also made a close alliance with the Somali Patriotic Movement (SPM), one of the two main factions of the Ogaden movement, headed by Colonel Ahmed Omar Jess, a former deputy commander in northern Somalia under Siad Barre in 1988–9. It was Colonel Jess who led the fighting around Kismayo. The other element that claimed and used the SPM label was headed by one of Siad Barre's former defence ministers, General Adan Abdullahi ("Gebiyu"), with his son-in-law Colonel Bililiqo. This faction was also based around Kismayo and allied with the forces of General Mohammed Sayeed ("Morgan"), who was a son-in-law of Siad Barre and commanded the forces of the Harti in and around Kismayo. The Harti are a grouping of three Darod clans, the Majerteen, the Dolbuhunta and the Warsengeli, in the Kismayo area where a number of families from these clans settled a couple of generations earlier and lay claim to Kismayo. General Morgan had retreated there after Siad Barre's flight to organize opposition to the USC. There is a third Nairobi-based faction in the SPM, represented by Omar Maalin who attended the Djibouti conference as the second vice-president to Ali Mahdi. His relationship with Colonel Jess was poor and little better with General Gebiyu. Nevertheless, he represents a political element in the SPM but has no armed forces.

After the March 1992 ceasefire in Mogadishu, General Aydeed's military activity originally concentrated against the other military forces and warlords operating to the south and west of the capital. These included the joint forces at Kismayo under General Gebiyu (Ogaden) as overall commander with Morgan (Majerteen) in charge of operations, seen as representing the fragile Darod alliance against the Hawiye. Although General Morgan's tough line in the north in 1988 and around Mogadishu in 1990 had not been forgotten, his presence in Kismayo was imperative because of the Harti. Their control around Kismayo fluctuated; on several occasions their forces advanced up the coast towards Mogadishu, and more than once captured both Merca and Brava. Equally, at one stage in 1991 Colonel Jess held Kismayo for a few weeks, and in July he even decided to try and emulate the Majerteen in the northeast and establish an Ogaden–SPM administration of Jubaland. This effort floundered for a number of reasons – his failure to consolidate his own position in the SPM, to rally the elements controlled by General Gebiyu, or in the last resort to maintain control of Kismayo. Nevertheless, quarrels between Colonel Jess's supporters and those of General Gebiyu helped to keep the town in ferment for months in 1991.

Generals Gebiyu and Morgan also co-ordinated activities with the Somali National Front (SNF), a largely Marehan grouping which aimed to incorporate all Darod clans. The SNF began by using Siad Barre's name to rally support – Siad had extensive amounts of funding still available – but this proved largely counter-productive except in Marehan areas. The SNF had a political leadership in Nairobi, headed by ex-defence minister General Omar Haji, and its military wing was originally organized by General Mohammed Hashi Gani (Marehan). General Gani, a former commander for Siad Barre in northern Somalia, had some successes. Moving out of the northwest in October 1991 his forces advanced to take Baidoa but were then expelled by the SDM with support from Aydeed. In January 1992, substantially resupplied with weapons, including tanks (some apparently bought from southern Ethiopia from ex-soldiers of Mengistu), he again took Baidoa and surrounded Balidogli, the airbase through which General Aydeed imported his *miraa* (*qat* – a leaf chewed to produce a narcotic effect which lasts for several hours) from Nairobi – the critical resource for control of his fighters, whom he could neither pay nor feed. There were no clashes at this stage, but there were reports that General Gani's men were exchanging weapons for *qat*.

The uneasy truce was broken in April 1992, when Siad Barre himself moved to Baidoa and pushed General Gani into advancing on Mogadishu. The calculation was that both General Aydeed and Ali Mahdi were exhausted and that General Aydeed was seriously weakened by sending fighters to help Colonel Jess at Kismayo. The move was premature. The SNF rapidly took Balidogli and pushed on to Afgoi only 30 km outside Mogadishu, but there, General Aydeed's men, buttressed in the emergency by other Hawiye fighters, including both Hawadle and Murasade, won a considerable victory. The SNF forces, split by disagreements over tactics, collapsed and were routed. Ten days later Siad Barre crossed into Kenya (and subsequently went on to Nigeria after President Moi made it clear he did not want him to stay); General Gani went north into Ethiopia. In early May 1992, Colonel Jess made another attack on Kismayo and captured the airport, but it was not until the middle of the month that he managed to take the town, with General Morgan retreating along the coast and then into Kenya.

The capture of Kismayo meant that General Aydeed's military position in the south and west looked unchallenged, but this was an illusion. Despite having substantial supplies of weapons, he did not make the progress he expected in establishing his authority when he pushed northwest after Siad Barre. He forced Siad out, set up his headquarters at Bardera, renaming his coalition the Somali National Alliance (SNA) in August 1992. His armed forces had taken the appellation of the Somali Liberation Army (SLA) earlier. He remained in Bardera for five months, returning to Mogadishu only in mid-September. This was, perhaps, in part a measure of his power when compared with Ali Mahdi, but it also reflected his difficulty in asserting his authority in the south and west. Bardera is a town close to the Marehan, Ogaden and Rahenwein clan territories, but Aydeed made little progress with any of them, failing to expand the SNA to attract more Ogaden or Rahenwein support or indeed to establish any real foothold in Marehan areas. This made his link with the SPM particularly important, as Colonel Jess had a significant force of several hundred experienced and well armed men, who are from the Mohammed Zubeir to which Colonel Jess belongs, and could provide a link to the Ogaden west and northwest of Kismayu. However, Colonel Jess comes from the Rer Adbilleh branch found around Degabour in Ethiopia, and his links with those in the Kismayu area are fragile; Jess also failed to build up satisfactory relations with the much divided Harti elders. Consequently, control of Kismayu remained uneasy.

This all meant that General Aydeed's control over the Mogadishu–Baidoa–Bardera axis and the south and west remained less complete than his military strength would suggest, as became clear in October 1992 after he had returned to Mogadishu. The weaknesses were almost immediately exposed when Bardera fell to a surprise attack by a combined force of the SNF led by General Ahmed Warsame, a former commander in northern Somalia under Siad Barre, and General Morgan's forces. With neither Colonel Jess nor General Aydeed there, Bardera proved vulnerable. The attack also coincided with operations by the SNF and the SSDF in central Somalia against the Habr Gidir which distracted Aydeed. Within two weeks the SNA counter-attacked towards Bardera. Announcing his intentions in advance, apparently to stop food aid going to the SNF forces in Bardera, General Aydeed dispatched a force from Baidoa to Bardera, including a number of his prized 54 tanks. Colonel Jess also advanced from the south with a force of about 800 men. They announced they had retaken Bardera on 26 October 1992, but by the end of the month it became clear that the SNF had succeeded in holding the town. There were reports that, immediately after capturing Bardera, General Morgan had laid mines around Bardera and that these had played a key rôle in denying access to General Aydeed.

The defeat of General Aydeed"s and Colonel Jess's forces opened the way to the SNF's advance on Kismayu which was pre-empted by the US intervention in December 1992, although a few months later a combination of circumstances allowed General Morgan's supporters to take control of the town and oust Colonel Jess's men. At Bardera, the SNF's disunited forces were believed to number about 3,000 men, while General Morgan was thought to have around another 750, though their condition only a few weeks earlier in Kenya had reportedly been very poor.

One of the more curious facets of the capture of Bardera was the resurrection of General Morgan as a political or military force. After his defeat at Kismayu and his retreat into Kenya in May 1992 Morgan was confined to Lamu by the Kenyan government. It was several months later that he was able to become active again when the Kenyans encouraged him to make an alliance with General Ahmed Warsame, the SNF leader in Gabahurrey. The SNF had moved back into the western border areas of Somalia almost as soon as General Aydeed had finished his successful campaign against Siad Barre in April. After discussions in September, Morgan was able to rearm his remaining forces and was provided with transport to Gabahurrey. How much support Morgan received from Kenya is unclear. General Aydeed was outspokenly critical of Kenya's rôle both before and after the loss of Bardera, particularly after the landing of a Kenyan military helicopter at Bardera in September 1992. At the very least, the Kenyan military as well as Somalis in Kenya's northeast province appear to have provided unofficial logistical support and to have allowed arms to cross the border. The SNF, well funded from Siad Barre's resources, appeared to be buying arms, mainly from private dealers. Kenyan support for the Darod, whether unofficial or not, appeared to owe little to policy and more to clan connections between Ogaden subclans in Kenya's northeast province and those in western Somalia. There were suggestions that some elements in the Kenyan establishment resented the overthrow of Siad Barre and the breaking of a number of lucrative business links with his regime and that this explained support for General Morgan and others. This was emphasized by the importance of the highly profitable *miraa* or *qat* trade. Miraa comes from Meru district in Kenya and is flown from Nairobi's Wilson airport to various small airstrips around Mogadishu and elsewhere, or to Mandera and other border points for onward distribution by road. It has been used by almost all the protagonists in Somalia to pacify their unpaid, often unfed, forces, though it renders their obedience to orders rather flexible. The trade has been calculated to be worth as much as $100,000 a day and would be extremely difficult to stop.

The other area of concern for General Aydeed before the US arrival was in central Somalia, where there had been a considerable number of clashes along the demarcation lines between the Habr Gidir and the Hawiye on the one hand and the Majerteen and the Marehan on the other. The two main areas of fighting were near the coast around Hobyo, General Aydeed's home area, and along the Chinese-built road east from Mataban and Dusa Mareb towards Galkayo, the headquarters of the Somali Salvation Democratic Front (SSDF) (Majerteen). The SNF (Marehan) forces were operating north of Dusa Mareb. The SSDF advance seized Hobyo for a time in August although it was soon abandoned again. Further east, the Habr Gidir were facing the SSDF between Dusa Mareb and Galkayo, and in mid-October were attacking villages just west of Galkayo.

General Aydeed's support among the Hawiye as a whole and the Habr Gidir subclans in particular remained essentially constant, though the impetus for peace within the Hawiye appeared to be receiving a boost towards the end of 1992. He certainly had the backing of his own Saad–Habr Gidir–Hawiye and of the 'Ayr–Habr Gidir–Hawiye but there were also questions about the manpower resources of these clans. Two other Habr Gidir subclans, the Salabaan and the Sarwi, were trying to organize Hawiye peace talks in an attempt to bring Aydeed and Ali Mahdi together, with little success. There were similar signs that Ali Mahdi's Abgal support was weakening, with some Abgal elders openly critical of his failure to make peace, and of his SNF alliance. All this led to greater efforts to try to influence the still unattached subclans and to weaken existing alliances. The Abgal tried hard to use the strains in the Hawadle relationship with General Aydeed, which included a clash at Mogadishu airport in November after the departure of the Irish president Mary Robinson when General Aydeed was refused permission to see her off. As many as 40 may have died in the fighting. This may have angered the Hawadle but they still appeared to find Ali Mahdi's links with the SNF more unpalatable. The Hawadle, like most of the Hawiye, do not want the Marehan or the Darod back in Mogadishu.

On the wider level, however, Ali Mahdi gained from the growing opposition to General Aydeed and the concern over his increased power in the south since May 1992. In Mogadishu itself, Ali Mahdi was careful not to break the ceasefire and calculated that he would gain more internationally from appearing to stand outside the conflict. He concentrated on trying to obtain other allies while, like General Aydeed, giving publicity to his calls for a reconciliation conference. Both refused to acknowledge the other's efforts, while claiming considerable support for their own. Ali Mahdi appeared to do better, and by using the 1991 Djibouti agreement as a basis for discussions he obtained an agreement with the SSDF. This included an immediate ceasefire between the Hawiye and the Majerteen, or rather between some elements of the two but not including General Aydeed's supporters; a call to strengthen unity with the elders having a special but unspecified rôle; the encouragement of free movement of goods and people; and the condemnation of "trespassing" in the territories of others. An SNF delegation attended the meeting as did the Egyptian ambassador who had played an important rôle in getting the talks under way.

A meeting between the SNF and Ali Mahdi followed in September, also attended by delegations from the SSDF and the SPM (General Gebiyu). In early October the process went a stage further when Ali Mahdi brokered a peace agreement between the SNF and one of the SDM factions. These meetings followed the previous pattern – agreements to iron out differences, the formation of committees of elders, co-operation over trade and movement of people, and condemnation of factions that indulged in bloodshed and aggression. In fact, Ali Mahdi had gone a considerable way to achieving a minimal consensus between the SSDF, the SNF and his own USC, or between the Majerteen, the Marehan and the Hawiye. The only real element that united them, however, was a fear of General Aydeed. There was no concrete indication of any progress in settling the feuds between Darod and Hawiye, although Ali Mahdi went to the Addis Ababa conference in March 1993 with the support of the SSDF, the SDM and the SNF.

One of the factors that helped Ali Mahdi in the latter part of 1992 was the increased significance of the United Nations and its assumption of a political rôle after the Algerian diplomat Mohammed Sahnoun was appointed the UN special representative in Somalia. However, the international body's own internal bureaucratic wrangling seriously hampered its effectiveness on the ground. Ambassador Sahnoun proved energetic, capable and competent in galvanizing UN aid efforts and, even more significantly, in winning the confidence of most leading political, military and traditional figures – a critical necessity in any peace process – and securing basic agreement for UN forces to oversee food distribution. The exigencies of his job demanded that Ambassador Sahnoun require the full support of the UN Secretary General, but this was lost in October 1992 by his criticism of the UN's activities in Somalia at the Geneva conference and, more publicly, on American television. His criticisms of the response of UN agencies to the Somali crisis as incompetent and his pointed questions as to why the World Health Organization was not operative after so many months won him few friends in the Organization and its bureaucracy. Equally, the Somali operation was the subject of bitter jurisdictional disputes and growing disagreements over responsibilities in the UN, particularly when it became clear just how large the UN's commitment in Somalia might become. Efforts to get UN troops deployed – the 500 sent to Mogadishu in August 1992 had still not been able to move by the first week of November – were bedevilled by the way the UN's New York headquarters insisted on control over field operations. Decisions were often delayed, sometimes indefinitely, as when Sahnoun and the commander of the UN forces Brigadier-General Imtiaz Shaheen asked for rations and uniforms for the clan militia fighters at the airport and the port in Mogadishu; the *quid pro quo* was to be agreement for the UN deployment at these points, but nothing was done.

In early October 1992 Ambassador Sahnoun launched the UN's Hundred Day programme in Geneva, essentially a relief programme calling for more food aid and provision of basic health services but also including the rehabilitation of civil society and, by extension, a significant political dimension. The programme was based on the report of a UN technical mission which went to Somalia in August 1992. The idea was that, alongside the UN forces, small security units of Somalis would also be deployed with the intention that they should later become the nucleus of a police force. In addition to the UN troops planned for Bosasso, Berbera and Kismayu, it was also made clear that political offices would be set up there to promote reconciliation at the regional level. The original intention was that a national reconciliation conference might be possible by the end of November or early December 1992 in Addis Ababa; in Geneva, Mohammed Sahnoun said that all factions, except the SNM in its self-proclaimed Republic of Somaliland in the north, had accepted the idea. Sahnoun also obtained widespread acceptance for the 3,000 extra troops called for by the UN Secretary General and agreed by the Security Council on 28 August 1992. The main exception was General Aydeed, one of the strongest critics of UN deployment, who believed that UN plans to cover security and food distribution, the highly optimistic "food for guns" idea, would boost Ali Mahdi's position. It had been Mahdi, in his self-declared position of president, who had actually requested the troops. In effect, General Aydeed claimed that the UN, in responding to the request, effectively recognized Ali Mahdi's legitimacy and authority which Aydeed refused to do. Aydeed was also worried by the open-ended nature of the UN commitment – 500 troops, rising to 3,000 with calls for up to 10,000 or even more.

He was not alone in this, but there was also growing pressure for the UN to deploy its forces to guard the food distribution and ensure minimal security with or without agreement. Sahnoun remained an advocate of the slow approach and of the necessity of proceeding on the basis of local reconciliation, and resisted quick deployment. But he was forced to resign at the end of October 1992 when his position became untenable after the Secretary General sent him a critical letter. Almost all of the international agencies deplored his resignation, as did Somalis from many different factions. *Africa Watch* referred to Sahnoun's removal in almost apocalyptic terms. In a rare display of unanimity, the permanent members of the Security Council were critical of the UN Secretary General for allowing Sahnoun to resign. In fact, some of the criticisms made of Sahnoun were valid. He did not always display even-handedness on the Somali political scene. There were some who felt that he was over-indulgent towards General Aydeed in his repeated refusals to allow the deployment of UN troops in Mogadishu and subsequently elsewhere. He was also criticized for his failure to appreciate the "reality" of the creation of the Republic of Somaliland in the north.

Sahnoun's failure underlined the UN's lack of decisiveness over Somalia and, more importantly, emphasized its weakness over how to end the conflict. There was a widespread feeling that the UN should use more muscle to ensure the success of an arms embargo and should close the Kenyan and Ethiopian borders. The UN presence in Somalia reinforced the pressure on General Aydeed and Ali Mahdi to talk peace, and both publicly committed themselves to a national reconciliation conference. However, the parameters of Somali political activity - conflicting and shifting clan allegiances segmented down to a local or village level, disgruntled warlords and politicians, shortages of resources, personal animosities - remained unchanged.

Some progress was made, with food aid beginning to make a real impact on the famine problem in some, but not all, areas; but it was still painfully slow. In the last resort the UN was simply not moving fast enough to satisfy its critics. It was this that persuaded Secretary General Boutros Boutros-Ghali to ask the United States to send in sufficient forces to ensure that aid deliveries would not be looted and would reach the starving. This task was simple enough to appeal to a US president in search of a high note on which to leave the White House. There was little thought to try to do more, though a wider rôle did prove inevitable. The US intervention, or invasion, as some preferred to describe it, did not satisfy everybody. It improved the delivery of large-scale aid, and cut back on the looting of food convoys and the activity of the "gunmen", though even on the humanitarian level it did not bring an end to famine or solve the attendant and far more critical medical problems. Nor, more significantly for Somalia's future, did it do more than scratch the surface of much needed disarmament of the major protagonists. This was one of the many tasks left to UNOSOM 2 (UN Operation for Somalia), which was left with a critically difficult job when it took over from the United States in April 1993. Besides realistically disarming the factions, it will have to organize political reconciliation. A start was made at the March 1993 conference in Addis Ababa, but many of the UN's critics argue that regional-level reconciliation is the primary necessity. UNOSOM 2 will also have to begin rehabilitation before any effective famine relief programme can work, by involving Somalis at all levels, using Somali professional skills to organize this effectively, and involving the traditional mechanisms of the clan elders. Above all, UNOSOM 2 will need time, patience, expertise, political sense and funds. Past experience suggests it will not deploy any of these in sufficient quantity to achieve real progress towards economic rehabilitation, peace or reconciliation.

Acknowledgements

The original version of this chapter was written as a report for Save the Children Fund. See P. S. Gilkes, *Ethnic and political movements in Ethiopia and Somalia* (London: Save the Children Fund, July 1992) and P. S. Gilkes, *Political events in Somalia/Somaliland* (London: Save the Children Fund, December 1992).

CHAPTER FIVE
Somaliland: birth of a new country?

GÉRARD PRUNIER

The collapse of the Siad Barre dictatorship in January 1991 has had very different consequences in the two ex-colonies that had linked up to create the Somali Republic in 1960. While the ex-Somalia Italiana exploded into violent fighting between various clans, the ex-British Somaliland moved into peace and impoverished independence with only a limited modicum of political turbulence. This chapter attempts to outline the process of change in the north, understand the shape and meaning of Somaliland independence, and evaluate the possible future of the area.

The domestic situation

While the last stages of the fighting in and around Mogadishu were unfolding, up in the north, most of the Awdal, North West, Togdheer and Sanaag regions and a good chunk of Sool were in the hands of the Somali National Movement (SNM). The guerilla organization, created in London in April 1981 by exiled members of the Issaq clan family, had been based in Ethiopia for a good many years, practising hit and run guerilla tactics, while political contradictions mounted and civil disobedience grew. President Mengistu, hard pressed by the war in Eritrea, had signed a peace agreement with Mogadishu in April 1988 in order to free his troops stationed in the Ogaden borders since the end of the 1977–8 war. Faced with the probability of being abandoned by its erstwhile ally, the SNM High Command opted for a daring dash forward and launched a simultaneous attack on several important towns. They were briefly occupied and then reconquered by government troops who mercilessly took revenge on the civilian population. Around 50,000 people were killed in a few days of intense artillery and aerial attacks, while 450,000 refugees streamed out of the urban areas and walked, under fire, all the way to Ethiopia.[1]

The reoccupation of the towns by the Mogadishu forces did not, however, lead to a general reconquest of the north. The government army remained penned up inside heavily mined perimeters and under constant siege by the SNM. Among the non-Issaq northern clans, whom the government used as auxiliaries, only the Gadabursi retained a fighting capability. The Dolbahante had been badly mauled in earlier fighting and the Issa tended to remain neutral.

The SNM functioned not as a guerilla "front" distinct from the population but rather as an armed expression of the Issaq people. This had good and bad effects. Among the strong points were a very democratic decision-making process, a real understanding of the ordinary people and a great resilience. Among the weak points one could note a tendency to confusion and lack of discipline and a general naïvety regarding the outside world.[2]

The main cities, including Boroma, Hargeisa, Berbera and Burao, still resisted the SNM but all fell within a few days of the collapse of Siad Barre's rule in Mogadishu in January 1991. Given the rôle played by the marginal clans[3] in the anti-SNM campaign, the SNM's behaviour in the very first few days of the takeover had a great importance for the possibility of future northern cohesion. If clanic revenge had been allowed to happen, the situation might well have evolved towards chaos as it did in the south. In fact, only a few Ogaden were shot on the spot after the occupation of Hargeisa; most were given SNM protection and eventually led back to Ethiopia. Boroma was taken over on 4 February 1991 with only 120–50 casualties. The civilian population fled to Ethiopia, but by the end of the month the Somali Democratic Alliance (SDA), the military organized arm of the Gadabursi, had reached an agreement with the SNM and most of the civilians returned.[4] Nevertheless, the SNM leadership felt the need to convene quickly a big *shir* (assembly) where non-Issaq leaders of the north would have the occasion to air their views and could be reassured about an uncertain future.

The evolution towards independence

The meeting took place in Berbera on 15–27 February 1991. It brought together the SNM leadership, various Issaq clan elders and representatives of the Gadabursi, Issa, Dolbahante and Warsangeli. Its most essential aim – to convince the non-Issaq clans that no revenge would be taken for their rôle in the war and at the same time to hear their feelings about the stance that should be adopted towards the south – was never officially expressed.

From the beginning the SNM was hostile to the unilateral assumption of power in Mogadishu by the Ali Mahdi wing of the United Somali Congress (USC). There were several reasons for this. The Ali Mahdi wing was a direct offshoot of the Manifesto Group,[5] which the SNM believed was ready to collaborate with the remnants of the Siad Barre regime still fighting in the south; they also felt that it was too close to foreign interests considered particularly inimical by northerners. Moreover, its independent assumption of power stood in violation of the tripartite agreement, signed by the SNM, the USC and the Somali Patriotic Movement (SPM)[6] on 2 October 1990, which provided for mutual consultation upon the fall of the dictatorship before any provisional government would be set up. The Berbera meeting gave the SNM leadership northern trans-clanic approval for its rejection of the Ali Mahdi government and agreed not to attend the meeting that was supposed to take place in Mogadishu on 14 March, declaring that "any northerner who would attend could not be seen as representing the northern region". For a movement that had called the appointment of Ali Mahdi as head of a transitional government "premature" and the appointment of Omar Arteh Ghalib as his prime minister as "preposterous", this was a definite political victory.[7]

More important, perhaps, the representatives of the non-Issaq clans had signed a document calling for a "revision of the Act of Union". The SNM was divided on the question of independence. A group close to ex-SNM chairman Mohammed Ahmed ("Silanyo") was definitely set against the idea because it feared foreign complications, and the new chairman Abdurahman Ali ("Tur")[8] was not far from sharing these views. But the pressure in favour of secession from the rank and file of the Issaq, both civilians and *jabhad* (fighters), was very strong. Calling for a "revision" of the Act left various avenues, including secession, confederation and negotiations for a federation, open at that stage. Non-Issaq clan support for the next move gave welcome leeway to a movement that had always operated in a very clan-conscious way and was careful to negotiate with clan elders rather than impose predecided views.

Various developments in early 1991 were to push the SNM and ordinary northerners further along the road towards secession. The first of these developments occurred while the February *shir* was still on. A combined armed force of ex-Siad Barre regulars and Issa militiamen took over the westernmost area of Awdal region. When Abdurahman Ali Tur and an SNM delegation went to Djibouti, they were told by President Hassan Guled Aptidon and his Secret Service Chief Ismail Omar Guelleh that the armed group was now called the United Somali Front (USF) and that the SNM should recognize its control over the Zeyla–Loyada–Garissa area.[9] The SNM chairman refused and moved militarily against the USF forces which were quickly defeated. The Issa component took refuge in Djibouti while the ex-Siad Barre soldiers, who were mainly of Majerteen and Ogaden origin, were shipped by sea back to Bossaso where they joined the recently reborn Somali Salvation Democratic Front (SSDF). The whole attempt had been quickly stopped but it made the SNM aware that, in the absence of any clear political decision, claims could be made to chunks of northern territory by almost anybody.

In the south, the situation was far from settled. Factional fighting had developed between the victorious USC, SPM and SSDF with ex-Siad Barre supporters joining in under the name of Somali National Front (SNF). Nevertheless, when he arrived in Djibouti on 15 March 1991, Prime Minister Omar Arteh spoke as if he represented a stable government and called on the SNM to negotiate. His approach enjoyed the support of the old pro-Siad Barre foreign lobby, because by early May 1991 Egyptian Foreign Affairs Under Secretary Sami Heyba and former Italian ambassador to Mogadishu Mario Sica flew to Berbera to push the idea of a "national" conference in Cairo. Among the SNM leadership, the feeling was growing that the forces that had organized the manifesto movement were now aiming at the restoration of their position under the Ali Mahdi banner and that, through them, southern domination could return. A broadened SNM central committee meeting was called to act as a general assembly. The existing central committee was enlarged by asking clan elders to choose additional representatives and a cross section of traditional leaders, businessmen and educated people (ex-civil servants, teachers) to assemble in Burao. On 15 May, without any prior discussion with the north, Mogadishu radio broadcast an announcement saying that the SNM had agreed to attend the proposed Cairo meeting. Feelings rose to a pitch and the delegates gave in to popular pressure, deciding on 16 May to repeal the 1 July 1960 Act of Union. Independence was declared to a cheering crowd on 18 May 1991.

The political aftermath

Immediately after the proclamation of independence, debates began on a new constitution. The constitutional committee was ethnically carefully balanced,[10] with the aim of keeping the consensus that had been achieved so far but leaving the final vote to the central committee. The main question of debate was whether to opt for a presidential or parliamentary regime. The former was chosen and Abdurahman Ali Tur became the first president of Somaliland on 26 May 1991 with Hassan Issa Jama as his vice-president. On 4 June the new cabinet was announced. Here again, the question of balance between the clans proved to be an essential preoccupation: out of the 17 ministers and 4 deputy ministers (including the president and vice-president), the lion's share went to the Issaq with 17 posts; in addition, 1 Warsangeli, 2 Dolbahante, 2 Gadabursi and 1 Issa were appointed. Among the Issaq, the various cabinet posts were also carefully distributed between the clans: 4 Habr Awal, 4 Habr Jaalo, 3 Habr Yunis, 2 Eidagalley, 3 Arap and 1 Ayub.[11]

The key minister portfolios were all in Issaq hands – Ismail Mahmood Hurre ("Buba") (Eidagalley) was appointed finance minister, Suleiman Aden ("Gal") (Habr Jaalo) became minister of the interior, former chairman of the SNM Yusuf Ali Sheikh Madar (Habr Awal) was appointed foreign minister and Mohammed Kahin Ahmed (Habr Jaalo) defence minister.

Foreign reactions to Somaliland's declaration of independence were rather muted. The OAU, in a communique issued from Abuja on 27 May 1991, asked the Somali authorities to reconsider their decision. Mogadishu's pro-

visional government and a few Arab capitals dismissed their "errant brothers" and Western governments kept silent. There were several reasons for
this, chief of which was the focus of diplomatic attention on the aftermath
of the Gulf war in Kurdistan and the disintegration of the Soviet Union.
Another factor was regional: the recent collapse of the Addis Ababa regime
had led to the *de facto* independence of Eritrea, and the general process of
reorganization in the Horn of Africa, torn by conflicts for the past quarter-
century, was unavoidable. In the short term, however, what mattered was
the increasing contrast between the violent developments in the south and
the maintenance of law and order in the north. This made the question of
defence organization and the transition from guerilla to regular army all the
more essential.

The army factor and the problem of stability

During the war the various SNM regiments had been organized on a strict
clanic and territorial basis from east to west, with the First Regiment being
entirely made up of Habr Jaalo, the Second Regiment of Habr Yunis, the
Third Regiment of Eidagalley, the Fourth and Fifth Regiments of Habr
Awal.[12] Each clan fought roughly on its own territory and elaborate pre-
cautions were taken when moving with weapons from one clan's area to
another. Combined operations were carefully planned to avoid clashes and
misunderstandings. The rare occurrences of inter-clanic murders were dealt
with quickly with sentences conducted by firing squad. *Uffo*, or sweet wind,
the only existing trans-clanic force, was made up of volunteers and remained small throughout the war but it was well respected and used for
dangerous missions.

After the declaration of independence in May 1991, the problem became
how to turn what had been an excellent guerilla force into a truly national
army and avoid the potential risk of the force disintegrating into a cluster
of dangerously parochial militia. Tensions quickly developed for a number
of reasons. During the summer of 1991 disarmament successfully began,
with many individual weapons being retrieved. Differences arose over the
fate of the "technicals", four-wheel-drive vehicles mounted with machine
guns and light artillery. Opinion divided between the President and his
allies on the one hand, and the Minister of Defence and his supporters on
the other, as to how to create a truly national trans-clanic army. Positions
became sharply opposed and a number of people, including some ex-SNM
worthies unhappy at being sidelined, moved to resurrect the old United
Somali Party (USP).[13] The Defence Minister felt that the Habr Jaalo, in
alliance with the Dolbahante and the Issa Musa subclan of the Habr Awal,
could swing things their way in a kind of eastern alliance against the western clans and he tried to obstruct the way of the "Codbur" force.[14] The
anti-presidential group accused Abdurahman Ali ("Tur") of inertia or even
of trying to sabotage the new independent government. Tur and his allies,

the Habr Yunis–Eidagalley–Saad Musa coalition, accused Mohammed Kahin of wanting to stage a coup. After some inter-clanic jockeying for power, the Defence Minister was pushed aside in November 1991 and replaced by Vice-President Hassan Issa Jama; both sides accused each other of stealing the funds generated by the Berbera customs. With revenues of about $700,000 per month, Berbera harbour was the only serious cash-generating element in the country, and the two groups competed for its control both as a tax base for the incipient state and for personal profit.

Under the new leadership, and that of Hassan Yonis who became chief of staff and the minister's technical adviser, the integration of the army was moved on by using material incentives, such as extra rations, for those willing to merge into non-clanic, non-territorial units. A number of fighters were also demobilized, but tensions rose sharply at the end of 1991 when Vice-President Hassan Issa Jama tried to use force. A number of dissenting ministers, including such political heavyweights as Suleiman Gal and Ahmed Ismail Duxsi, were dismissed. On 2 January 1992 fighting broke out in Burao between pro (Habr Yunis) and anti-government (Habr Jaalo) forces and lasted for four days. Clan elders, including non-Issaq northern clans such as the Gadabursi and Dolbahante, intervened immediately to stop the confrontation. The civilian population obstinately refused to be dragged into the conflict at the clan level. Even those hostile to President Abdurahman Ali Tur's government were yet more hostile to the idea of a military coup. A muddled situation of part-time fighting and part-time negotiations dragged on for the first half of 1992. Berbera harbour changed three times in bouts of short sharp fighting. Finally, dissident forces under Colonel Ibrahim "Dega Wayne" reoccupied the harbour on 9 August 1992 and a peace accord was signed in Sheikh in November of that year, under the sponsorship of the Somaliland *Gurti* (assembly).

A slow process of normalization followed, during which the administration of Abdurahman Tur was progressively marginalized. Between 22 January and 24 February 1993, a nationwide *shir* was called in Boroma. The choice of location was deliberate: Boroma, the Gadabursi "capital", was chosen to show the minority clans that they could share fully in the political process, even if the Issaq dominated it, both by sheer numbers and as a result of recent history. President Abdurahman Tur was not even present during most of the meeting, being ostensibly on diplomatic trips abroad, mainly in Egypt. By the time the council ended, he was president in name only and his administration had become highly theoretical. Nevertheless, in early March when he offered to resign he was rather abruptly told to stay on. The reason was external. The predominantly US forces of the UN International Task Force (UNITAF) had pulled out of southern Somalia and a new UN operation called UNOSOM 2 was underway. In New York, Secretary General Boutros Ghali was pushing for the armed mandate of the international body to be clearly extended to the whole of ex-Somalia's territory, i.e.

including Somaliland. There had been vigorous demonstrations in various Somaliland towns against foreign armed intervention, and SNM leaders who were then carefully engineering the refocusing of the national leadership did not want the UN to be able to point to a leadership crisis in the breakaway state in order to justify intervention.

On 5 March 1993 a second *shir* was called in Boroma, in order to select a new national leadership. About 150 official, and many more unofficial, delegates attended. The meeting lasted until 20 May and represented a good example of the Somali decision-making process. There were two main candidates, Siad Barre's ex- foreign minister Omar Arteh Ghalib and Mohammed Haji Ibrahim Egal, British Somaliland's brief prime minister and the architect of Somalia's unity in 1960. Abdurahman Ali Tur remained as a ghost candidate but was never seriously considered. Omar Arteh is a Habr Awal Issaq of the Saad Musa subclan. Ibrahim Egal is also a Habr Awal, but from the Issa Musa subclan. In any case, the Habr Yunis–Arap–Eidagalley clanic coalition which had run the first administration was slated to go. Despite the very marginal clanic differentiation, clan was not a main issue in the "election", but many other things were. The long Boroma *shir* was a marvellous opportunity to air a lot of old quarrels, bad feeling and rank stories. A lot came out into the open. People shouted at each other. Poetry was written and recited, a very essential element in public Somali life. Some other people were made fun of. Quarrels were resolved through public excuses, arranged marriages and exchanges of ceremonial gifts, all concurring to *hal*, the compensation of honour so important in Somali culture. In a way, one could say that electing the new president became almost a side issue and that the political and cultural display of social dynamics became essential. Ibrahim Egal had understood this very well and adopted a very reserved posture. His rival, on the other hand distributed lavish gifts of cash, air tickets to Mecca and embroidered scarves. In the end, he got barely 20 votes to more that 100 for Egal. Many of the Habr Yunis delegates had withdrawn, sulking, before the vote. Their absence was commented on with irony, although their refusal later to take up the ministerial position Egal had slated them for (including defence) is a sign that they will want some kind of compensation for losing the leadership and that they could prove to be troublesome in the future.

The whole process lasted little short of three months, but, in spite of the Habr Yunis Eidagalley bad humour, resulted in a consolidation of the leadership situation. Almost immediately, local administration started to be organized not only in Berbera, but also in Erigavo, Burao and elsewhere, which contrasted with the old neglect of practical matters too often displayed by President Abdurahman Ali Tur. Egal's old British connection was brought back into play and stabilization of the internal situation began to look like a feasible target.

The economic situation

The dominant fact of the Somaliland economy is an almost total destruction of the whole infrastructure.[15] Not only was there war and its corollary, a complete lack of maintenance of civilian installations, but there was a systematic looting and destruction of everything left standing. This had two causes. Siad Barre's army was not paid, and therefore resorted to pillaging in order to survive; everything with the slightest cash value was dismantled (door and window frames, electrical and plumbing fittings were pulled out, underground pipes dug up, power lines taken down for use as scrap metal) and sold in the markets of Egypt and the Gulf states. Clan hatreds, particularly of the southern Darod for the Issaq, led to the systematic destruction of what could not be removed. In 1990, I saw the damage done to the electrical lines that used to supply the Geed Deble water pumping station.[16] Every single pole along the entire line had been knocked down with a tank, a vindictive and militarily useless gesture since the government still held the town of Hargeisa at that time. Such senseless destruction was everywhere in evidence. The only major infrastructure left intact at the end of the war were the tarmac roads, since those had been used by government forces.

Even the social infrastructure was targeted: 77 out of 87 schools were destroyed in the northwest region, 51 out of 55 in Togdheer and 34 out 37 in Sanaag.[17] The result was to take the country's economy back half a century or more. There are no longer any working hospitals, no postal service or telecommunications and very limited public transport. Whatever electricity or running water is available is the result of local private initiatives. One of the gravest impediments to a return to normal life are the several thousand landmines scattered by the ex-government army and the SNM. Their locations are vaguely known and accidents are a common occurrence.[18] Demining, undertaken by a private British company financed for a while by the EC stopped in 1992 because of the lack of funds. The French army in Djibouti, contacted by the Somali authorities, were ready to help, but were unable to obtain the green light from Paris.

Another major problem linked with the destruction of the infrastructure is the return of 400,000 refugees filtering back from camps in Ethiopia. The insecurity that has developed in eastern Ethiopia since the Ethiopian People's Revolutionary Democratic Forces (EPRDF) takeover in May 1991 makes it difficult for the United Nations High Commission for Refugees to operate. On the other hand, moving refugees back "home" is somewhat theoretical because most of their homes have been destroyed.[19]

Given the story of extreme underinvestment in the north during the Siad barre years,[20] and given the thorough looting of any fixed plant during 1988–90, the economy is essentially based on cattle raising and export. In fact, even in the old united Somalia, cattle exports from the north had been the main source of foreign exchange.[21] It is only from taxes on cattle exports and customs duties that the new fledgling state can expect to build a minimum tax base. The embryonic civil service is currently paid only in kind (food rations).

The ambiguous diplomatic status of Somaliland is a major stumbling block in getting foreign aid. France, which built the 175,000 ton per year Berbera cement plant, was approached to help in its rehabilitation, but declined to look into the matter pending diplomatic recognition. The same problem plagues the question of oil exploration; several companies (Sunoil, Conoco, Chevron) had exploration programmes in the north but these contracts were signed with Mogadishu and their legal status is now in doubt. So far, the only foreign interest in Somaliland has come from another potentially diplomatically ambiguous territory, Hong Kong. A delegation of Hong Kong businessmen visited Somaliland in October 1991 and promised help in various ways including water system rehabilitation and air transport training, but the implementation of this offer might prove to be difficult.

The diplomatic situation

The regional perspective

The main diplomatic question for Somaliland has been to define its position in relationship to the south, where the general principle of avoiding active interference has not precluded having friends. In 1989 the SNM made contact with General Mohammed Farah Aydeed when he abandoned his post as ambassador to New Delhi in order to breathe a bit of military fire into a then very prudent civilian USC. Later, the northern leaders kept a preferential link with General Aydeed because they saw him as the only resolutely anti-Siad Barre force among the Hawiye. Indeed, many of their clan elders were trying to work with the Manifesto Group in order to reach a compromise with the dictatorship which the SNM judged to be either impossible if a minimum democratic standard was adhered to or amounting to treason if it worked. The hasty takeover of Ali Mahdi's Manifesto faction of the USC after the fall of Mogadishu confirmed their worse fears, especially when a considerable number of ex-Siad Barre associates resurfaced in and around the provisional government.[22]

After the repeal of the June 1960 Act of Union and the aborted Cairo conference, a new conference was organized for 15–26 July 1991 in Djibouti (largely with the same sponsors). The choice of location was unfortunate and the Somaliland authorities refused to attend. The ethno-political arrangements agreed in the conference resolutions were referred to by President Abdurahman Ali Tur as "practically unworkable". They in fact did not work, and the fighting continued unabated.

At the popular level, the situation in the south is often viewed by the north with a mixture of indifference and glee – indifference because northerners are more concerned with their own day-to-day survival, and glee because "the southerners are getting a taste of what we have had to live with during the past 10 years, because of them". The attitude of the northern authorities is both more open and more embarrassing. The unending civil strife in the south is viewed as a source of shame for all Somalis, and despite sympathy for General Aydeed, only limited help has been extended. (Some ammunition was sent in November 1991.) There remains a hope that a link with the south can be re-established when Mogadishu reaches some form of political equilibrium. But the resolve never to leave again the fate of the north in southern hands is equally strong. Offers of a share in an eventual central government, as envisaged by the July 1991 Djibouti conference, are seen as unrealistic, and a Confederation of Equals is the preferred form of relationship when the long term is envisioned.

The Republic of Djibouti has posed a problem for the SNM since 1981 when it was founded. One reason was the kind of awe with which President Hassan Gouled Aptidon viewed his counterpart in Mogadishu. General Siad Barre had been a key factor in the Djibouti independence process during the 1970s and then a looming force over the border, even after his defeat at the hands of Ethiopia in 1978. As a result, Djibouti was never a safe haven for the SNM, which preferred to use Dire Dawa as a window on the outside world. After 1988, when the guerilla movement began to control most of the countryside,[23] the border was closed, causing considerable economic hardship to northern Somalia and Berbera, which was in government hands and was commercially dead. Although the hardship affected Djibouti itself, for which northern Somalia had long been a more profitable economic hinterland than Ethiopia, the cross-border trade ban was maintained for several months after the overthrow of Siad Barre's dictatorship in January 1991.[24] After the failure of the annexation attempt in March 1991 relations remained sour, and the hosting by President Gouled of the July 1991 "reconciliation conference", sponsored by the very forces the SNM considered the most unfriendly (Egypt, Italy and the Ali Mahdi wing of the USC), did nothing to improve the situation or further the prospect of north–south talks. This led Somaliland to welcome a delegation from the Front pour la Restauration de l'Unité et de la Démocratie[25] in October 1991, a gesture perceived by President Gouled as a breach of Somali solidarity.

The relationship with Ethiopia is complex, and the fall of President Mengistu in May 1991 gave it a new direction. For the Issaq, as for all Somalis, Ethiopia was the traditional enemy. When the SNM had been created in 1981 it had been a rather conservative organization with a leadership of merchants and former civil servants, while Ethiopia was at the height of its Marxist–Leninist fever. Nevertheless, tactical interests led the SNM to come to Ethiopia at the invitation of the then President Mengistu. After the failure of the Balambale–Goldogob SSDF's 1982 invasion attempt, Mengistu began to loose faith with the southern and mostly Majerteen opposition. The increasing efficiency of SNM operations in the north led him to switch his support to the Issaq front. But the Ethiopian help was of course strictly tactical and linked to Ethiopian interests. In April 1988 Mengistu decided to sacrifice the SNM in favour of his reconciliation with Siad Barre. Even if the northern movement eventually managed to turn the situation around to its own benefit (at the enormous cost of the May 1988 massacres), this served as a reminder that Ethiopia could be friendly, but should never be completely trusted. Mengistu's fall has not fundamentally altered this view, and the new government is looked upon with prudence. Issaq camel herders have been going deep into the *haud* for the past few years[26] and their main interest is to keep free access to pastures. The EPRDF regime in Addis Ababa seems unlikely, both because of its weakness and because of its official policy of ethnic federalism, to object to the traditional exercise of grazing rights into Ethiopian territory. Somaliland has so far managed to stay clear of the Oromo–Issa clashes which have taken place in northwestern Ogaden and shows every sign of trying to avoid entanglement in the probable future ethnic strife in Ethiopia. The rejection of the "greater Somalia" ideology is deeply felt and the Issaq, who once supported it enthusiastically, trace their problems to this period and accuse Siad Barre of having used it as an excuse for the exploitation of the north. In this respect, Somaliland seems to want to go back roughly to the situation in 1910 when the official border with Ethiopia was nothing but a line drawn on the map which existed for the mutual satisfaction of the British Colonial Office and the Emperor Menelik alone and left the local populations largely undisturbed.

To conclude this review of Somaliland in its regional context, one must mention the looming shadow of the Arab world. The Arab League and several of its main members (Egypt, Saudi Arabia, Oman) had sided with Siad Barre in 1977. At the time, he was seen as a "born-again Arab brother" who had just broken with Moscow and was fighting a Christian power (Ethiopia) which was backed by communists. The support for Mogadishu outlasted the 1978 defeat and went on throughout the years of the civil war.[27] It is this legacy that is at the root of today's extreme prudence of the north when dealing with the Arab world and all the more so since the Gulf states are such an important source of foreign exchange through the remittances of expatriate Issaq workers.[28]

In the Arab world, special mention has to be made of Yemen and the Sudan. Yemen, for reasons of cultural, geographical and historical proximity, is not a truly "foreign" land for the Somalis. Aden remained quite sympathetic to the SNM during the war years and today hosts a quasi-Embassy of Somaliland; contacts with Berbera are frequent. Sudan, under its Islamic fundamentalist leadership, remains something of an unknown quantity.

What is clear is that the Somalis have their place in Hassan el-Turabi's dreams of an "Islamist caliphate". Symbolic quantities of medical and food aid were sent by Khartoum after Somaliland's May 1991 declaration of independence; but in the July 1991 Djibouti conference the Sudanese delegation tried to force the hand of the Hargeisa authorities in making them reunite with the south. This move was looked upon very coldly by President Abdurahman Ali Tur, who was then in Khartoum at the invitation of the al-Bashir government. In December 1991 the Sudanese regime announced that it would host a "Somali reconciliation conference" but this declaration has so far not materialized. Throughout 1992 the attention of the Sudanese Islamist movement shifted from the north to the south where opportunities for political influence appeared better. After its defeat at Bossaso in mid-1992, the Islamist forces that had tried to wrest control of the Majerteen country from the SSDF took refuge in the Las Khoreh–Erigavo area in Somaliland. Given the state of unsettled political authority prevailing at the end of 1992, the authorities maintained an uneasy truce with them, and Khartoum, although sympathetic, did not actively offer them support.

The international perspective

The international environment in which the proclamation of Somaliland independence occurred was contradictory. On the one hand, the *de facto* independence of Eritrea, a move almost officially sanctioned by the United States, was discreetly backed by the Arab countries and evoked widespread sympathy in Europe which created a powerful regional precedent. A nearly bankrupt Organization of African Unity (OAU) could do almost nothing against it. On the other hand, the disintegration of Yugoslavia and the USSR made European powers wary of granting diplomatic recognition to new states. This, added to the loss of strategic interest in the Horn of Africa resulting from the disappearance of communism as a world force, created a situation in which nobody wanted to hurry. There was no hostility towards Somaliland but no special sympathy either. Washington and the various European capitals also wanted to see how the war in southern Somalia would finally end before undertaking a diplomatic move which they felt could prove to be premature in the case of a north–south reconciliation. The December 1992 US-sponsored international intervention in the south, resulting as it did in no clear political reorganization, has provided an added incentive for the international community to wait. Nationally, the situation in the north has two basic dimensions. First, *vis-à-vis* the south, the trauma of the war years is too deep and the fear of possible renewed southern dominance too strong for reunification to hold any appeal for the Somaliland population. This reality is often difficult to apprehend for the southerners who have kept alive the dream of a "Greater Somalia" through the whole process of unbridled southern anarchy. Secondly, some sort of political equilibrium more stable than the one that has prevailed since January

1991 is a necessary precondition for international recognition to take place. Thus, the present state of diplomatic limbo (February 1994) might continue for some time, although, from the points of view of international law and political consciousness, the situation somewhat resembles that of Eritrea.[29]

Union with "mother Ethiopia" was a popular slogan in the 1940s and 1950s, and the separate colonial domination that had given this segment of the nation a different historical consciousness could have been overcome by an understanding and open-minded government. Instead, bigoted attitudes and abstract centralist policies succeeded in driving that part of the nation back into the consciousness of its own separate identity. There are two modern concepts of the nation state: one is the Germanic concept of Herder, rooted in its notions of *blut und boden* (blood and soil), emphasizing a shared organic inheritance; the other is the Latin concept illustrated by Ernest Renan and based on *la volonté de vivre ensemble* (the will to live together), which makes a nation the result of a conscious historical process. Partly inherited and partly the process of an ongoing creation, culture stands as a mediator between these two concepts. Somaliland has recently chosen the path of Renan after experimenting with the path of Herder. It remains to be seen if the heritage of Somali culture that it shares with the south will prove in the future to be a strong enough bond for some new form of common consciousness to emerge, or if Somaliness will prove to remain as elusive a political concept as pan-Arabism.

Notes

1. For a well informed treatment of that crisis, see "Somalia: a government at war with its own people", *Africa Watch Report* (1990), 268.
2. For an eyewitness assessment of the SNM in its last year of war, see G. Prunier, "A candid view of SNM", *Horn of Africa* 14 (1992).
3. "Marginal" of course only in relationship to the mostly Issaq north. From their Boroma base the Gadabursi had kept the strongest fighting spirit on the government side. But armed Ogaden refugees of the 1977–8 war played a major rôle in garrisoning the other towns. Their exactions against the civilian Issaq population, even *before* the May 1988 slaughter, left a strong legacy of bitterness.
4. The main peacemaker was Colonel Abdurahman Ahmed Ali, nicknamed "Farid Tol Wayaye" (the warrior without a family) because he was the only SNM commander of Gadabursi origin. After the reconciliation his nickname changed to "Farid Laba Tol Ley" (the warrior with two families).
5. The Manifesto group was made up of merchants and professionals who tried, in the last days of the Siad Barre regime, to find a compromise with the declining dictatorship in order to ensure a non-military transition. While one of their purposes was to minimize violence, they also wanted to salvage a number of financial and political interests. They enjoyed discreet Italian and Egyptian support and were opposed to the USC wing led by General Mohammed Farah Aydeed, who stood for pursuing the war against the Siad Barre forces to the bitter end.

6. This was the organizational arm of some of the Ogaden clans, led by the ex-military commander of the Hargeisa garrison, Colonel Omar Jess. It fought mainly in the southernmost region of the country around Kisimayo.

7. Omar Arteh is an Issaq. He had been Siad Barre's foreign minister and presided over Somalia's admission to the Arab League, a move considered detrimental to the north because of the support Arab states eventually gave to the dictatorship during the civil war. Later arrested by Siad Barre, and even condemned to death, Omar Arteh was pardoned and made prime minister in a last-ditch attempt at "national reconciliation". But he had already lost any credibility in the north and his confirmation as prime minister by provisional President Ali Mahdi was perceived as an extension of Siad Barre's clumsy attempts to woo the Issaq.

8. He had been elected chairman of the March 1990 Congress of the Movement. "Silanyo" is a Habr Jaalo while Abdurahman Ali Tur is Habr Yunis. The movement's deputy chairman Hassan Issa Jama, from the Arap clan, had stayed on. However, clan identity, while very important in other political respects, had nothing to do with pro- or anti-independence views.

9. This area is mainly populated by Issa. The aim of the Djibouti government was to annex it to the small republic in order to increase the number of Issa voters in the legislative elections that were then due to take place in the spring of 1992 but were subsequently delayed until 1993. Since the La Baule speech by François Mitterand in 1990, pressure had been emanating from Paris for greater democratization, and President Guled feared that he would be forced into an open multi-party election. Given Afar opposition to his rule and growing disaffection among Djibouti's various Somali clans, a massive Issa population intake, consisting of people grateful for the improved standard of living offered by Djibouti citizenship, appeared to be a good recipe for electoral success.

10. The 45 Issaq members were balanced by 20 Gadabursi, 25 Dolbahante, 10 Warsangeli and 5 Issa.

11. For a detailed breakdown, see J. Drysdale, *Somaliland 1991* (Hove: Global States Ltd, 1991).

12. The existence of two regional regiments was not due to any demographic superiority of the Habr Awal (in fact, they are less numerous than either the Habr Jaalo or the Habr Yunis) but rather to the mistrust of the Issa Musa and the Saad Musa subclans of each other and their preference to fight in separate units.

13. This party had been created in British Somaliland in early 1960 to defend the northern Darod and Dir interests because the majority Somali National League (SNL) was Issaq-dominated. For more details, see I. M. Lewis, *A modern history of Somalia*, pp. 148–78 (London: Longman, 1980).

14. "Codbur" (bumpy forehead) was the nickname of a legendary fighter who had led a daring commando attack inside Hargeisa during the war to free some detained SNM officers. He later died of natural causes in an Ethiopian refugee camp and his name was given to the first inter-clanic force centrally organized after the end of the war.

15. The best assessment of this tragic situation can be found in the report compiled by the Inter-Non-Governmental Organization Committee for Somalia: V. Coultan, R. Davies, N. Mariano, *A report of the assessment mission to northern Somalia* (London: INCS, 1991).

16. Built by Chinese technical aid, this was a major installation which provided water for the city of Hargeisa.

17. *A report of the assessment mission . . . .* , 63. Such vindictiveness goes a long way towards explaining the secessionist feelings of the north.

18. For a very good assessment of this tragic situation, see African Rights and Mines Advisory Group, *Violent deed live on: landmines in Somalia and Somaliland* (London, December 1993).

19. The refugees are in their overwhelming majority town dwellers from Hargeisa and Burao. The nomads (65 per cent of the Somaliland population) are mostly all right; but the refugees could not live with them.

20. Only about 6 per cent of industrial investment undertaken in Somalia during those years was located in the north. For the best account of the industrial situation, see Drysdale, 36–8, 57–60.

21. Northern exports (mostly to Saudi Arabia) represent roughly $50–$60 million potential. Transport and banking are now the main problems. Telefax links via satellite are now in operation but they are expensive.

22. One could mention Ahmed Gilao, former head of the dreaded National Security Service, Abdullahi Ahmed Addow, former finance minister, Hussein Kulmiye Afrah, Barre's former vice-president or Mohammed Sheikh Osman, another former finance minister and millionaire who was elected to the USC central committee.

23. The SNM occupied Loyada, thus extending effective control along the Djibouti border in early 1989.

24. The reason was essentially political; see note 9.

25. This was a Djibouti opposition movement, mainly made up of Afar, even it did address the whole spectrum of public opinion. In fact, the Issaq and Gadabursi Somalis in Djibouti tended to sympathize with the Afar rather than with their Issa Somali brothers because of the predatory politics of Gouled's Mamasan Issa subclan.

26. Their main problem in the area in the early 1980s was between the Mogadishu army and the Western Somali Liberation Front alliance with the Ogaden clans against them. They had won, partly with regular Ethiopian army help. See G. Prunier, "Structures de clan et pouvoir politique en Somalie", *Cultures et Développement* **17** (1987), 692–3.

27. The Hawker Hunter fighter–bombers used to raze Hargeisa had been supplied by the United Arab Emirates, which also for a while paid the salaries of their South African mercenary pilots.

28. Drysdale, 19–20.

29. Of course, the "national characters" of Eritreans and Somali do create significant cultural differences between the two independence political processes. For an interesting assessment of the Somaliland case, see Ahmed Yusuf Farah & I. M. Lewis, *Somalia: the roots of reconciliation. A survey of grassroots peace conferences in "Somaliland"* (London: Action Aid, 1993).

CHAPTER SIX

Sudan: a new political character?

PETER WOODWARD

Like many observers of Sudan, my feelings of recent years have been increasingly pessimistic. In the mid-1980s I wrote a paper entitled "Is Sudan governable?" and then moved to the even more fundamental theme, "Is Sudan in a terminal state?" Few have seriously doubted the state of decay that the country, like several others in Africa, has been experiencing, although the analyses of causes have varied.[1] There have been attempts to address the issues from Sudanese political quarters, notably the "New Sudan", for which the Sudan People's Liberation Army (SPLA) fighting in the south has proclaimed that it has been struggling.[2] But it has not been the SPLA that has had its chance to create a "New Sudan": rather, the opportunity for a self-proclaimed revolutionary transformation has fallen to a group of Islamic fundamentalists who have at least had a major influence on government since the seizure of power by the last successful military coup in June 1989. This chapter is an attempt to try to assess broadly the extent to which those now in power appear to have "broken the mould" of Sudanese politics, or how far even their experiences represent less a revolution than a continuation of themes in Sudanese politics.[3]

My own past analysis had not suggested that Sudan was likely to be transformed by an essentially ideological grouping, be it communist or Muslim Brotherhood (the two major ideological movements in modern Sudanese history) in origin. The obvious route to "revolution" is for such movements to capture the state and then use its power to transform society to the particular ideological blueprint of the movement. However, while capturing the state via a coup has proved possible, controlling society has been more difficult. The state itself has limited capacity, and its ability to impose the views of its rulers on such a vast country as Sudan with a heterogeneous population (now over 25 million) has always been limited.[4] Political control has never been that assured to any regime, and since independence in 1956 there has been a succession of unstable civilian and military governments. My own view has been that even relative stability has involved the capacity to deploy a mixture of social bases involving elements of class (where intra-elite rivalry is generated for the perquisites of the state), religion (in particular the capacity of Islamic movements partially to transcend ethnic and class divisions) and ethnicity (which as in much of Africa is still a dynamic force).[5] Essentially modern ideological movements (including the Muslim Brotherhood) have what I saw as inherent limitations for such political manoeuvrings. They lack the kind of ethnic and religious links that could spread their influence widely into Sudanese society (in the north at least). In terms of class, they might build a body of support (communists from workers, Muslim Brothers from commercial expansion among the petty bourgeoisie) but the base would remain fairly narrow. In addition, an overtly ideological movement would arouse the hostility of other ideological claimants. Thus, the questions that arose for me were how was a regime actively supported by the Muslim Brotherhood, otherwise known as the National Islamic Front (NIF), able to overcome what I had seen as the inherent limitations of its situation, and to what extent had the revolution it proclaimed proved possible?

Certainly the proponents of the regime called it a revolution: the National Salvation Revolution. But then, Sudan had had revolutions before (most notably the May Revolution of 1969 which produced some change), although arguably scarcely major or lasting ones. In addition to the self-proclaimed aims of the soldiers who took power, an academic study by a sympathizer that appeared shortly after the coup, entitled *Turabi's revolution: Islam and power in Sudan*, took its title from the leading part in the growth of the Muslim Brotherhood that has been played by Dr Hassan el-Turabi.[6] Revolutions are about change; indeed, the degree and speed of change may be how revolution is defined. A coup is not a revolution: it is what happens afterwards, and how different the situation becomes, that will be judged in deciding whether a revolution has taken place.

In seeking to assess this, four main issues will be addressed. First, did the coup of 1989 open up a situation that made it notably different as an experience of military intervention from those Sudan went through after the coups of 1958 and 1969? Secondly, has a self-proclaimed ideological revolution pursued a clear ideological path? Thirdly, has the state itself been restructured in a revolutionary manner? And fourthly, what is the revolutionary character of the regime's policies?

The coup of 1989

To be in Sudan in the weeks before 30 June 1989, when the coup that brought the new regime took place, was to be aware of the widespread speculation of a coup, so bad was the working of Sudan's restored Westminster style liberal democracy. The question seemed to be less whether there would be a coup than when and whose coup it would be? But that was not new. In 1958, immediately before the first coup by General Abboud, there was widespread dissatisfaction with the convolutions of democratic govern-ment; and in 1969 a coup was being widely canvassed before it occurred. On neither occasion did the possibility of such a coup persuade the squab-bling politicians to behave as anything other than lemmings. In 1989 there were some signs of concern, and there was pressure on Prime Minister Sadiq El Mahdi to negotiate with the SPLA, but the rumours of a likely coup abounded nevertheless.

Once the coup had taken place, the question came to focus on the kind of military-civilian relations that would evolve. The two previous successful coups sooner or later embarked on informal relations with politically signifi-cant segments of the civilian society, in an attempt to broaden the base of the regime. In the case of President Abboud after 1958, it had been later rather than sooner. Nevertheless, his regime did informally come to terms with one or the other, and sometimes both, of the major Islamic move-ments, Mahdists and Khatmiyya. Likewise, President Nimeiri's regime began with an association with the Sudan Communist Party, and in his 16 years in power he was to be allied at one time or another with all major movements, except for one wing of the Unionist Party. Nevertheless, these were only alliances. The army as an institution appeared to maintain an identity of its own, albeit wracked by internal factional feuding and on occasions further attempted coups against the existing military leader. At the same time, the movements maintained an autonomy and were never re-garded as merging with the regime. The military could discard the political movements, and the movements could distance themselves from the mili-tary regime.

The regime that took power in 1989 was immediately scanned for alle-giances. The names were fairly obscure since they were mainly middle-rank officers, led by one Brigadier Omar Hassan al-Bashir. Some, who were par-ticularly astute, immediately picked up on the hidden hand of the NIF in the coup, while others admitted that, although some appeared to have an Islamist background, others of the new regime did not. But whatever the balance of pre-coup allegiance, it has become apparent that the regime's major ally in civilian society is the NIF. What is less clear is whether this is a continuation of the old pattern of military civilian alliance, or whether it heralds a new politicization of the military.

If indeed the coup was NIF-inspired, as many now allege, that in itself was not particularly novel. All parties have had their supporters within the army; similar accusations have been levelled after past coups. The Mahdist-backed Umma Party encouraged Abboud's intervention in 1958; and com-munists were involved in Nimeiri's 1969 coup, though there is argument about the attitude of the Sudan Communist Party (SCP) immediately prior to the coup. NIF supporters in their turn had spoken of their faction in the army before June 1989.[7]

What is of greater significance after the coup is the extent to which the army remains an institution in its own right, or has been penetrated by the NIF. If it retains its own institutional identity and awareness, then two possibilities follow. One is that the present military regime leaders at some time or other will seek to make their own political moves towards breaking with the NIF or diluting NIF influences by bringing in others to give a broader political base. There have been rumours of such talks and negotiations, but Sudanese politics abound with rumour and it is difficult to know how much credence to attach to such reports. The second possibility is that a group of military figures will mount their own coup in an attempt to break the current links between the existing military rulers and the NIF. There have been numerous alleged coup attempts which suggests differing views within the army, but there have also been mass purges of those considered unreliable amongst the officer corps. Estimates put the number purged at between 600 and 2,000 (the latter figure representing 40 per cent of the officer corps).

Another uncertain element in this equation is the creation of the Popular Defence Force (PDF). The force was established by the al-Bashir regime after it came to power in June 1989 allegedly to augment the army. Anything up to 150,000 people, many of them youths, have been enrolled and given weapons and a fairly brief military training, as well as being subjected to fundamentalist propaganda. The PDF's official purpose is to protect the National Salvation Revolution and it has been deployed in the civil war in the south. Reports suggest that, because of the ideological commitment of at least some of the PDF, it was used prominently in the 1992 dry season offensive, and that it took significant casualties. The PDF is clearly an additional coercive instrument *vis-à-vis* Sudanese society; what is less clear is any political repercussions they may have for the regime. In particular, is the PDF meant to act as a political counterweight to the army should the latter seek to revert to its rôle as an independent actor in Sudanese politics? If this is intended, how great is the PDF's capacity, and how great a weighting should it be given in considering the vulnerability of the present regime not only to another uprising from below (of the kind that overthrew Abboud in 1964 and Nimeiri in 1985), but to any form of action that might weaken the NIF from within the military? (I am omitting the possibility of the PDF itself being an independent political actor since it is too new, and too little is known of it to make any such speculation worthwhile.)

No regime in Sudan's years of independence has shown such a concern with security as the present one, and all the evidence suggests that this includes military as much as civilian security. But whether that means that "the military" has one way or another been neutralized remains to be seen. In addition to the factors mentioned above, account must also be taken of the impact on the army of continued civil war in southern Sudan. Until 1992 the army had seemed to be losing ground. But with military support from Iran, following a visit by President Rafsanjani late in 1991, which included training, arms and the money to buy new equipment from China, the army and the PDF were able to make major advances in the south against the Sudan People's Liberation Army (SPLA) which was itself weakened by factional infighting. Thus, by the end of 1992 the danger of trouble within the army as a result of continuing setbacks in the civil war appeared to have been allayed.

Tangentially, it is also worth considering the impact of security on civilians. It is said that four or five security networks are now in operation, and their impact is substantial, with arbitrary arrests, disappearances, detention without trial, torture and killings. In scale and ruthlessness, nothing like it has occurred in Sudan since the Mahdist state of the late 19th century. Yet its impact is hard to gauge. Much has been heard of it since its target has largely been the Western-educated elite and former politicians, picked on for obvious ideological and political reasons. But to what extent it has created a police state as far as the mass of the population is concerned is harder to estimate. It has acted harshly against shanty towns around the capital by deporting thousands to more remote ill equipped sites; but at the same time, reports suggest that ordinary criminality, amongst the urban communities at least, continues to rise, fuelled by continuing and possibly growing economic hardship. However, faced with an outbreak of urban protests in October 1993, the PDF was able to take swift and effective action to disperse the demonstrators.

A revolutionary ideology?

I began this chapter with a discussion of the 1989 coup, because the coup is a well established feature of Sudanese political life, and discussion of it is central to regime survival. However, the coup backers would doubtless claim that the central issue is the pursuit of the ideology of the NIF. This gives rise to the question of what the ideology of the NIF actually is and whether it is being implemented in ways that depart dramatically from developments hitherto.

Clearly, there is meant to be a revolution and an interpretation of Islam is central to it. As el-Affendi's book makes clear, the NIF was out "to make a bid to control the state and impose their norms on society and hope to succeed where their opponents have failed by defining a new Sudanese community based on Islam".[8] However, the precise nature of this ideology is hard to gauge. Undoubtedly, the leading ideologist has been Dr Hassan el-Turabi, the British and French educated Sudanese law lecturer who has a very individualistic approach. While influenced by figures such as Hassan el-Banna and Abu el-Ala el-Maududi, Turabi believes in formulating his own interpretation of Islamic fundamentalism based upon his own understanding and application of first principles. Such a view has been anathema to those who take a more juristic or sufi approach to Islam from the outset. However, for many years Turabi was not given to the production of a major treatise and thus his views on many subjects have emerged in a rather piecemeal way. Moreover, his views were not unchallenged by other Muslim Brothers nor, of course, by Muslims outside the Brotherhood.[9] As studies of Turabi's record have also made clear, he is extremely pragmatic, thus making uncertain how far an assessment of his ideological views are indicative of his likely course of action.

In these circumstances it is more appropriate to look at the record of government since 1989 from the standpoint of enactment of ideology, and in particular at what an assertion of an intention to pursue "authentic Sudanese traditions and culture" has meant in practice. A central issue has been that of *shari'a* (Islamic) law, and especially the *huddud* punishments (amputation, floggings, etc.). In this field the new regime was following a well trodden path. Islamic law had been on the agenda of Sudanese political discourse for many years before September 1983 when Nimeiri suddenly introduced it, to acclaim from the Muslim Brotherhood, and then went on an orgy of *huddud* punishment. Following his overthrow there was a period of uncertainty, with talk of Nimeiri's September Laws (as they were often called) being withdrawn, while the *huddud* punishments were effectively in abeyance. There was even a moment in 1989 when it appeared the *shari'a* might be withdrawn to facilitate peace with the SPLA; and, as already mentioned, some believe that it was this prospect that precipitated the coup of 1989. However,, it was not until early 1991 that the new regime finally brought *shari'a* out of abeyance, and even then its pursuit has been mixed. While the whip has been quite freely used, the practice of amputation has been much less frequent thus far than under Nimeiri (though this may be due to past Muslim Brotherhood disputes about *huddud* punishments).[10]

The sense of something less than a clear revolutionary ideology is also apparent in the large congresses called to decide on Sudan's direction, at which many of those invited to attend are not known as committed Muslim Brothers. In the autumn of 1991 no less than 4,000 "experts" were assembled to a Conference on a Comprehensive Strategy at which they were invited to chart the course for the Sudan to the year 2000. At the same time, and apparently unrelated to this conference, a new stricter code pertaining particularly to women (dress, office conditions, etc.) was suddenly promulgated. Such developments make it unclear how far there is a hidden ideological agenda unfolding; how far a small group are taking ad hoc and/or pragmatic decisions on ideological matters; and how far there really is a degree of ideological doubt in the regime which would be receptive to some inputs from Sudanese society more generally.

The corollary of this ideological revolution is the extent to which it is impacting on the thinking of Sudanese. Sudanese Islam has long been seen as of a relatively tolerant character, and as *sunni* rather than *shi'a* and less fanatical in character. Nonetheless, Sudan was the country of the great revolt of Ahmed El Mahdi in the 19th century, and after his death the Khalifa Abdullahi imposed a far-reaching Islamic state. There appears to be an innate recognition in northern Sudan of appeals to Islam and the *shari'a*. It is tempered, however, by a recent history of tolerance and by doubts about the legitimacy of the present rulers, especially their displacement of the leadership provided for so long by Sudan's holy families, such as the El Mahdi, al-Mirghani and Hindi families and followers. It is part of NIF thinking that modernization from independence until the late 1970s and the social uprooting caused by the civil war and environmental crises of the 1980s have left Sudanese society in a more malleable condition than hitherto. It is difficult to come to any conclusion, but it is one factor that would be relevant in any estimation of a possible *intifada* (uprising) of the kind that took place in 1964 and 1985. These successes owed much to the security shortcomings of regimes as well as to popular protest, and, as discussed earlier, the present rulers may have learned these lessons.

A new state?

Perhaps the major change in the structure of the state has been the adoption of federalism. The debate about federalism in Sudan is not new: at the time of independence in 1956 it had been conceded to worried southerners that there would be consideration of a federal constitution, though this was soon jettisoned in post-independence constitutional deliberations.[11] There has also long been discussion of an Islamic constitution to which federalism has in practice largely been the counterpoint of constitutional debate.

Instead of federalism, whose failure of implementation was associated with the periods of multi-party rule (1956-8, 1965-9), the regime of ex-President Nimeiri pursued regional government, first in the south from 1972 and then throughout the country from 1980. The regime that seized power in 1989 has essentially built on that experience in introducing its own brand of federalism rather than making a wholly new start. Thus, the new states announced were very similar to the old regions, although the provincial structure below them was altered. However, in January 1994 a wide-ranging review of the state structure, officially in the name of further decentralization, led to a total of 26 states being established.

But if the idea of federalism is less than revolutionary, how far has the practice altered? Under Nimeiri regionalism in reality contained few major devolved powers. The regions were to nominate three candidates for the governorship from which Nimeiri would select one. In practice, he had to take account of ethnic factors, especially when there were demonstrations against his proposal to appoint a non-Darfuri to Darfur. At the same time, the local tax base and/or collecting capacity was so weak that heavy financial reliance on the centre persisted. (It was largely to improve revenue collection that there was a return in the mid-1980s to the old system of native administration at the local level.)

The new regime appears to have gone along largely with what it inherited. There are new governors, but, like their predecessors, they are appointed by the centre, and so far without even a choice from local nominees. Thus, in reality they are regarded, first and foremost, as men acceptable to the regime. The state ministers have also been nominated by the central government to ensure the loyalty to the regime of the new governor.

The commitment to federalism is put in doubt not only by apparent practice thus far, but by the reorganization of local administration. In place of the old districts, there is now a smaller number of provinces in each state of the federation. Reports suggest that many of the new provincial commissioners – appointed from the centre – owe their positions as much to religious conviction as to administrative experience. Whether that will make them effective arms of the Islamic Revolution or ineffective would-be transformers of the Sudanese countryside remains to be seen; doubtless, some will be more successful than others.

At the same time it appointed political administrators, the regime also unfurled a new "democratic" system to encourage popular participation, but without a return to the previous multi-party system. This is to be achieved through "basic congresses", which represent local communities. Power is supposed to flow up from them through council, province and state levels to the National Congress. It is notable that no special emphasis appears to have been put on the state level in spite of its being a federal system. At the state level the congresses are linked with sectoral groupings, described as "women, youth and students, social and cultural, and economic" as well as by "basic state constituencies"; while the National Congress also has a direct sectoral and national constituency input. The system outlined has obvious ideological parallels with Libya (from which it is in part derived), as well as some structural overtones of the Sudan Socialist Union (SSU) of Nimeiri's years. Yet neither comparison is one of dynamic grass-roots participation, but rather of situations in which local elites have generally been able to adjust and manoeuvre to retain their existing influence in the new structures. Reports of the "basic congress" elections at the start of 1992 also point to a lack of success of those candidates associated locally with the NIF, leading to a raising of the quota of appointed members to ensure at least a degree of NIF influence at local levels.

Overall it remains unclear how planned these structural changes have been. Federalism may have been little more than an attempted sop to the three southern states to allow them to opt out of *shari'a* law, while provincial reorganization and the system of congresses could be an attempt to fuse central government influence with local participation at the community level. Taken together, the changes pose potential administrative and political questions that are hard to determine, but which will be significant if Sudan's "Islamic revolution" is to bring a far-reaching transformation. It should also be added that as far as finance is concerned there appears to be as much reliance on the scant resources of central government as ever; and thus the vital element of financial autonomy upon which some real prospect of state and local autonomy might be built is still largely missing.

At the same time as the state has been restructured, there has also been a considerable shakeout of personnel. There may well have been some reason for these dismissals: Sudan's civil service in particular has long been overmanned, inefficient and often corrupt. A slimmer more efficient set of government departments, perhaps accompanied by the privatization of the equally unsuccessful parastatals of various kinds, can be seen as making sense. However, there is a considerable feeling that the slimming of the state is less an administrative reconstruction than a piece of political adjustment. Thus, those who went were not necessarily the most incompetent and corrupt, while those who have taken over have often been, in effect, regime appointees, including in several cases young and inexperienced NIF members. The continuance of corruption is still widely alleged, as is the accusation that the privatization program affecting parastatals has been intended to pass into the hands of NIF businessmen the economic assets of the state at knockdown prices. If this is correct, then, far from producing more efficient services and facilities, inexperience and greed could result in performances even worse than hitherto.

Such a move to "politicize" the state is, however, not entirely new. On an earlier occasion, when the overtly ideological Communist Party was central to a military regime (1969–71), there was a similar scenario. Then it was the conservatives and Islamists who found themselves dismissed, while the "commanding heights" of the economy were nationalized. Now it is the secularists and leftists who are being targeted for exclusion while denationalization is one of the routes to political control of the economy.

Policies

The area of policy that has caused most concern outside Sudan has probably been human rights. Respected international bodies such as Amnesty International and Africa Watch have regularly catalogued the abuses, including arrest and detention in very poor conditions without trial, executions with a scarcely credible judicial process and the use of armed militias to commit atrocities on civilians in the course of the civil war. All this is in addition to the view often expressed that *huddud* punishments under *shari'a* law are themselves contrary to international conventions to which Sudan is a signatory.

I would certainly take the view that Sudan's human rights record since 1989 is the worst that the country has experienced since independence, but how far this is a wholly new phenomenon and how far a worsening of longer-term trends is less clear. Sudan's long experience of civil war included some gross abuses of civilians as far back as the mid-1960s, while armed militias terrorizing civilian populations have been a marked feature of the second civil war from the mid-1980s. Detention without trial occurred under Nimeiri's regime, as did beatings and other forms of abuse. And, as already mentioned, *huddud* punishments involving amputation were far more frequent under Nimeiri than they have been since 1989.

Along with Islamic law, the pursuit of "authentic Sudanese traditions and culture" has centred on culture and education. Yet here too, the question remains how much is revolutionary and how much an intensification of earlier trends. One of the most dramatic moves has been the introduction of virtually instant plans for the Arabization of higher education, but the subject is not new. It has been discussed for years in Sudan's universities, and creeping Arabization has been ongoing, as illustrated by the presentation in Arabic of numerous theses for higher degrees in the Faculty of Arts of the University of Khartoum. Perhaps a more crucial test will be the determination to press ahead quickly even in problem areas such as the natural sciences. There are reports of attempts to accompany Arabization with a selection of texts that will effectively limit the academic freedom of university teachers in faculties such as arts and social sciences. (Meanwhile English still retains an important place in the curriculum in the schools and there are even some plans to extend its teaching.) As well as the Arabization of higher education, Islamization also seems to be promoted. In particular, the theme of the "Islamization of knowledge" has been put forward, extending even into the natural sciences.

The situation with academic staff has appeared to worsen steadily. It would be expected that, as in the civil service, the "Islamic revolution" would target secularists and leftists in universities, and in a number of instances this has happened from the outset. Over time, however, more and more respected apolitical academics have also been forced out, often in obscure circumstances, and reports puts the total at 84.[12] At the same time as academics have been dismissed, detained, tortured and forced into exile, there have been hurried attempts to appoint and promote staff connected with the Muslim Brotherhood.

In addition to staff, students have come in for strong repressive measures. Early 1992 in particular saw a forcible confrontation in which deaths occurred amongst the student body and there were further confrontations at the end of 1993. New students are now required to go through a rigorous program of military training and ideological indoctrination before proceeding to their studies. At the same time, there have been measures taken to encourage the return of those studying overseas. In Egypt there have long been many thousands of Sudanese students, but financial support for them from Sudan has now been cut which forced many to return home. The creation of new regional universities to take them, as well as new generations of students, has been announced, but thus far the staffing and facilities appear to be very limited.

Government-funded universities in Sudan have long been centres of opposition to successive regimes, and it is understandable, if not condonable, that the present rulers would wish to contain that threat. However, in the steps outlined above there is the danger that they are now going further to attack the academic and intellectual premises on which the universities were built, which ensured, at one time, the international reputation of the University of Khartoum as a leading centre for higher education in Africa and the Middle East.

On the cultural front, there has been a general pursuit of Islamic culture through the state-controlled media, but a similar development occurred during the last years of Nimeiri's rule. More "revolutionary" have been the attempts to regulate the social and working conditions of women, including at the end of 1991 new dress codes. However, how far these new codes are being enforced remains unclear; as with *huddud* punishments, there may be a considerable gap between theory and practice.

With regard to the economy, the developments of the late 1970s have largely continued. Thus, the "Islamization" of the economy through the banking and credit system is not new, and was itself an important aspect of the rise of the influence of the Muslim Brotherhood. Perhaps the most innovative aspect of this regime has been the attempt to extend credit to small businessmen starting up in local communities, when hitherto it had been large- and then middle-scale operations that the banks had targeted. How far this is a purely economic policy and how far credit is once again being targeted in a way intended to develop the regime's political base is hard to tell. In any case Sudan's overall economic position remains as parlous under this regime, in spite of considerable propaganda efforts, as it was under its predecessors. The Islamists may be just as much perceived as milking what they can from the economy by controlling currency, commodity markets, foreign trade and aid, as did those who ruled before them.[13]

The pursuit of the Islamic revolution has contributed to the continuance of civil war. The efforts to pursue peace, particularly those involving former US President Jimmy Carter, revealed clearly not only the gap between the new regime on the one side and the Sudan People's Liberation Army (SPLA) on the other, but also the lack of serious intent to seek to bridge it. Both seemed as intent on their own different agendas as on any serious efforts at negotiation and compromise (while the government has sought to exploit the splits in the SPLA since 1991). Depressing though this has been in view of the horrendous social costs of the war, as well as its continuing drain on Sudan's economy, it too is an intensification of past failures. Since 1985 and Nimeiri's downfall, there seems to have been a history of failed peace-making efforts. Although there are those who argue that the 1989 coup was staged to prevent what was about to be a breakthrough, the deal had not actually been accomplished. The most that can be said is that Sudan was closer to peace immediately before the coup than it has been at any time since; however, that is no guarantee that peace would have been accomplished but for the present rulers.

In foreign policy the regime has become identified with an aggressive Islamic "revolutionary" stance that has isolated it from more conservative regimes in North Africa and the Arabian peninsular. Publicly, Sudan was associated with support for Saddam Hussein during the Gulf war as well as with a growing, if exaggerated, relationship with Iran. The regime has also projected its close political relationship with its neighbours in Chad, Ethiopia and Eritrea; though there is an ambivalence here, since it also seeks to promote Islamism (as was demonstrated in Somalia in 1992), which could be perceived as threatening the stability of the Ethiopian and Eritrean governments in particular. Frequently it is alleged that Sudan has become a centre for promoting the Islamic movement in North Africa by training potential terrorists with Iranian assistance, and acting as a conduit for money, arms and propaganda. But this too is not so new; the combination of the slide into civil war, the pursuit of Islamic fundamentalism, economic collapse and general political incompetence throughout the 1980s had long left Sudan increasingly isolated and marginalized. Little more than super-power rivalry in the Horn of Africa accorded it greater importance, and that too has now passed from the scene. Thus, Sudan seeks to star as the first modern Islamic regime in the Arab world while, at the same time, looking for financial and economic aid from tho very Western institutions and Arab Gulf states to whom its supposedly radical Islamic policies are anathema.

Conclusion

It was natural for Sudan's new ideologically motivated rulers to speak of "revolution", though they were not the first to do so. For years after the 1969 coup, Nimeiri proclaimed his May Revolution. Similarly, it was natural for Sudan's old politicians and the many who have decided to leave Sudan to proclaim it a revolution, albeit rejecting both its Islamic credentials and the success of its policies. I would certainly concede that things have changed; my uncertainty lies in assessing the extent and importance of those changes.

Contrary to the expectations of many people, the regime that seized power in 1989 has not only survived, but appears to have consolidated itself. Certainly it appears to maintain a firmer grip on the state, while its opponents are in growing disarray. Perhaps this is not after all so surprising if one remembers the years of preparation of the Muslim Brotherhood and its long infiltration of the state and penetration of the institutions of the economy, during which time the old parties, whether in government or opposition, were in decline. What is less clear is how far a "revolution" from above has been attempted, or is possible. As far as the attempt is concerned, this chapter has tried to question whether the measures taken have been new, or merely the intensification of processes that have been at work for a longer time. Ideologically, Islamism in various aspects had been promoted for years; organizationally much groundwork had already been laid. Despite controlling the state and intensifying the Islamic "revolution", it is questionable how much can be achieved by the government. The efforts to win over small businessmen have, despite the regime's use of the banks and its attempts to concentrate Sudan's economic resources in the hands of its supporters, been handicapped by the country's economic and debt crisis. Its structural weakness is so desperate that trumpeting some short-term achievement, such as a better harvest, is no indicator of recovery. Bereft of resources, and with accelerating inflation, there is little with which to win support. Education and the media may be used for Islamic Orwellianism, but while the quantity of the former may have expanded, its quality is widely believed to be in sharp decline. Coercion may repress opposition, but it is hardly likely to cement the state in place, especially in such a heterogeneous and historically lightly governed country. International isolation will not make the task any easier, and although there might in time be further Islamic regimes in the region, their wider international position and collective solidarity would still be uncertain.

The question also remains of how clear a revolutionary agenda the regime ever had. Certainly the best known ideologist, Hassan el-Turabi, never published a clear-cut credo, and was noted far more for his organizational and tactical ability than the comprehensiveness and coherence of his ideology. If it is thus essentially a movement to gain and consolidate power, first within Sudan and then possibly for Islamism more broadly, then it may survive for the foreseeable future; but the depth of its foundations in Sudanese society will remain comparatively shallow.

Notes

1. P. Woodward, "Is Sudan governable?", *British Society for Middle Eastern Studies Bulletin* (1987),.

2.   SPLM/SPLA Department of Information, "On the new Sudan". In *Management of the crises in the Sudan*, A. Ahmed & G. Sorbo (eds), (Bergen: CDS, 1989).

3.   I had hoped to make this assessment at first hand but was not able to got to Sudan as planned in September 1991.

4.   In spite of (or perhaps because of) the size of its civil service, Sudan has been a typical "soft" Third World state.

5.   P. Woodward, *Sudan 1898–1989: the unstable state* (Boulder, Colorado: Lynne Reiner, 1990).

6.   A. el-Affendi, *Turabi's revolution: Islam and power in Sudan* (London: Grey Seal, 1991).

7.   Comments of this kind were made to me personally by NIF supporters.

8.   El-Affendi, p. 163.

9.   El-Affendi, Chapter 9,; T. Niblock, "Islamic movements and Sudan's political coherence". In *Sudan: history, identity, ideology*, H. Bleuchot, C. Delmet, D. Hopwood (eds), 253–68 (Reading: Ithaca Press, 1991).

10. El-Affendi, p. 163.

11. M. B. Hamid, "Devolution and national integration in Sudan". In *Sudan since independence*, M. al-Rahim et al. (eds), 121–42 (Aldershot: Gower Press, 1986).

12. "Sudan: violations of academic freedom", *Africa Watch* **4**.

13. More comment on the economy in particular is in Roland Marchal, "Le Soudan entre islamisme et dictature militaire", *Monde Arabe Maghreb Machrek* **137** (1992), 56–79. An earlier survey of developments appeared in *Middle East Report*, September–October 1991.

CHAPTER SEVEN

Sudan's political and economic future: a southern perspective

Bona Malwal

The past few years have been momentous for the Horn of Africa. In May 1991, Ethiopia achieved a feat, perhaps second only to that of Uganda, of driving away from the seat of government a regime that had been in power for more than a decade and a half. The fall of the Marxist regime of Colonel Mengistu Haile Mariam came only a few months after the demise of the international mentor of communism, the Soviet Union. The victory of the revolutionaries in Eritrea and Ethiopia also made history of a different sort, giving birth to the new nation of Eritrea out of the barrel of a gun. The Ethiopian People's Revolutionary Democratic Front (EPRDF) and the Eritrean People' Liberation Front (EPLF) had joined forces against the Mengistu regime with the fullest understanding that, when Mengistu was gone, they would no longer maintain the unity of Ethiopia by force of arms and that the Eritreans would decide freely whether to remain in the union or secede. The decision was never in doubt. The Eritrean people, who had fought for nearly 30 years to achieve self-determination for their country, would surely opt for independence.

As events were unfolding in a positive way for those who struggled against Mengistu and the Ethiopian establishment, another struggle in the Horn of Africa, that in Somalia, was not going so well. Another regional dictator, General Mohammed Siad Barre, had been driven from the seat of government in Mogadishu, but the process of replacing him did not go as smoothly as it had in Ethiopia. The people of Somalia, known throughout Africa for the homogeneity of their language and culture, had turned on each other in the aftermath of Siad Barre's departure. Warlordism ravaged the Somali countryside. The lawlessness and carnage this produced made it Africa's first good case for a large-scale international military and humanitarian intervention, which eventually took place with Operation Restore Hope in October 1992. So horrific were the television scenes transmitted from Somalia that many on the continent and beyond came to feel that the intervention perhaps came 11 months too late.

For me personally, and perhaps for most southern Sudanese, these events in the Horn of Africa were of such a mixed nature that the advantages and disadvantages were extremely difficult to discern clearly. If the Somalis, a homogeneous people, could get into such disarray, how could southern Sudan, a highly heterogeneous tribal society which has fought for more than three decades to uphold its African racial and cultural identity *vis à vis* the threat of Arab and Islamic racial and cultural assimilation, hold together as a state? On the other hand, most southern Sudanese took some comfort from the fact that Eritrea, which, like southern Sudan, is also a tribally heterogeneous nation, had for all practical purposes become an independent state after the overthrow of the Mengistu regime. This meant that, despite the Organization of African Unity's charter, which seeks to discourage any changes in post-colonial boundaries or the breakup of its member states, the door for the creation of new states in Africa had become ajar if not quite totally open. It becomes a question for those struggling for a similar cause to copy the Eritreans and fight for independence on the battlefield.

Long before the Eritreans won militarily against Addis Ababa in May 1991, the only two cases that qualified for opting out of the Organization for African Unity's (OAU) stand for the infallibility of colonial borders were Eritrea and southern Sudan. Many will argue that the two cases and situations are not similar, but few would not accept that each case was strong in its own right and for its own reasons.

While the situations in both Ethiopia and Somalia have some general bearing on that of Sudan, events in Ethiopia in particular had a more direct impact. The two countries are direct neighbours, with long-standing connections between their peoples and between their two governments. In addition to the traditional impact of refugees fleeing to neighbouring countries to escape long-running civil wars, each country has long suspected the other of supporting its internal rebels. During the first civil war in Sudan, Ethiopia was one of the neighbouring countries that offered generous refuge to tens of thousands of southern Sudanese. It was in Ethiopia, with the help of the late Emperor Haile Selassie, that the 1955–72 civil war between northern and southern Sudan was ended in a negotiated peace agreement which gave southern Sudan regional autonomy in 1972. After the Addis Ababa agreement, southern Sudan even had to set up a temporary Amharic school in Upper Nile Province to accommodate the southern Sudanese schoolchildren repatriated from Ethiopia at the end of the war. Emperor Haile Selassie visited the southern Sudanese capital of Juba in March 1973 to join the Sudanese people in their celebrations marking the first anniversary of the end of the civil war.

Emperor Haile Selassie and the Ethiopian establishment felt that they had helped Sudan end its civil conflict and heal the wounds of war. It was therefore not unreasonable, from Addis Ababa's point of view, to expect Khartoum to help Ethiopia end *its* civil war. Instead, the popular belief in

Ethiopia was that Khartoum was in fact supporting the rebels against Addis Ababa in all sorts of ways. Because Khartoum had done little, or perhaps could do little, to help Addis Ababa, Colonel Mengistu gave sanctuary to the leadership of the Sudan People's Liberation Army (SPLA) in what was seen as a tit-for-tat action. The enemy of one's enemy became one's friend.

The impact of Mengistu's support was considerable. Almost overnight, he gave the SPLA an international legitimacy that would have been difficult to achieve in any other way. Colonel John Garang de Mabior instantly became, thanks to Mengistu's sponsorship, an acceptable leader to much of black Africa. Garang's ideas of a "New Sudan" had gone down well in Africa, particularly with Mengistu. The Ethiopian regime was fighting the Eritreans in a separatist civil war of its own, so there would be no support if the southern Sudanese movement were to take a separatist position. Garang's call for a united New Sudan in which there would be equality of opportunities for all was a comfortable proposition for Addis Ababa. The southern Sudanese rebel leader was welcomed both for what he represented and for the manner in which he represented it. Little wonder, therefore, that Mengistu's friendship with Colonel Garang brought problems for the SPLA once Mengistu was deposed.

Unity or separation

With Colonel Mengistu out of power in Addis Ababa, both the internal and the external contradictions of the southern Sudanese movement inevitably came to the surface. The "Nasir coup" of 28 August 1991 by three of Colonel Garang's former colleagues in the high command of the SPLA threw the whole debate about the future of southern Sudan into the open. Commanders Riak Machar, Lam Akol and Gordon Kong staged a well publicized announcement in which they declared that they had overthrown Colonel Garang and taken control of the SPLA. They were helped considerably by the fact that the BBC's correspondent in Nairobi, Colin Blaine, flew to Nasir on a United Nations relief plane especially to record the coup announcement. The three commanders declared further that they intended to negotiate the separation of southern Sudan from the north. While they were making these declarations over the BBC, Colonel Garang was, in fact, sitting comfortably more than 400 miles away in Torit in eastern Equatoria with the remaining 10 members of his 13-man High Command still very much with him. The world did not know this because the BBC did not wish to disclose the full story. The BBC's influence around the world is such that, regardless of the truth on the ground, the Nasir version became the reality on the airwaves.

In June 1993 the Nasir faction remains a reality in the southern Sudanese equation but its leaders have amended their ambitious plans. When their coup against Colonel Garang failed on the ground, they opted instead for what they now fondly call "a crippling revolution" that is intended eventually to engulf the whole of southern Sudan.

In practical terms, the Nasir revolt has been a tragic disaster for the southern movement. The fall of Mengistu, which seemed to trigger it, would alone have been enough to traumatize the south, given that Addis Ababa, the friendliest capital in Africa to southern Sudanese, had been transformed overnight into the friend of their worst enemy, Khartoum. The added burden of an internal rebellion caused many people to think that the southern movement would not survive.

Internally, traditional tribal contradictions and rivalries surfaced, further weakening the south. The Nasir group sought to highlight old fears within the south about Dinka domination of the politics of the region. If you tell a non-Dinka southerner that your programme is to get rid of the Dinka John Garang and then liberate the south under a non-Dinka leadership, you might gain some adherents. However, the reality on the ground makes it impossible to totally exclude the Dinka, or any other tribe of the south, from the equation. It was more expedient to say that the only problem is John Garang, thereby attempting to divide the Dinka by isolating one section from the rest of the tribe. So the Nasir leaders targeted the Bor Dinka, assuming that they would win over other sections of the Dinka. The tactic sometimes works, especially when, as often is the case, there are disgruntled political opponents within the tribe. But disgruntlement is not confined to one tribe and it is not a very credible basis for political alignment.

It was understandable that those who had suffered long years of detention under Colonel Garang, who were released partly if not wholly as a result of the Nasir rebellion, would join forces with the faction in the so-called united SPLA. Although these internal divisions had a devastating effect on the unity of the southern Sudan movement, the defeat predicted by the doom-mongers has failed to materialize since the August 1991 coup.

Regardless of the claims and counter-claims about who has what forces under his command in the now highly divided SPLA, it was clear that the common enemy of the south – the Islamic Fundamentalist military dictatorship in Khartoum, led by Lieutenant General Omar Hassan al-Bashir and under the control of the National Islamic Front (NIF) party of Dr Hassan el-Turabi – knows full well who its real opponent is in southern Sudan. The regime knows that Garang still controls the more effective military force, and he is the opponent they wish to undermine and to confront. It is interesting that, while on the one hand the Nasir group loudly proclaims its support for separation and accuses Colonel Garang of seeking a unity settlement with the north, it is actively and openly co-operating with Khartoum. Khartoum, on the other hand, continues to claim vehemently that it has never been prepared to consider separation for the south. Co-operation between Khartoum and the Nasir group is perhaps the best indication of how threatened both feel by Garang's military force, even though they try to minimize this in their propaganda. Nasir's close co-operation with Khartoum and its military reliance on Khartoum's support betrays both its own separatist claims and Khartoum's assertion that it will have nothing to do with separatists. While it may be obvious that Khartoum is bent on weakening the south in whatever way possible, so that any final settlement of the conflict will entail minimal concessions, it is less clear how the Nasir group believes it can reach a separation deal with Khartoum once it has collaborated with it against the mainstream SPLA.

Most enlightened southerners can see that separation could not be negotiated with the north, but has to be fought for and won in the battlefield. It is ironic that commanders who had fought the north, for six years in the case of Riak Machar and four years in the case of Lam Akol, were now trying to negotiate what they had failed to win on the battlefield. Most southerners are dismayed by the clear fact that the Nasir coup has weakened the south's ability to pursue its just cause. Khartoum might have succeeded in damaging its opponents in the south, but it still needs to answer the just case of the south politically. Even the unlikely event of an outright military victory will never solve the political grievances at the centre of the civil war. So what is Khartoum's answer to the south?

Islam and militarism

There is little doubt that the al-Bashir regime has only one solution to offer the south – an Islamic fundamentalist agenda – which it is quite prepared to impose by military force. It was clear from the day the regime seized power in a military coup in June 1989 that it intended to bring the whole country under control according to a strict Islamic and Arab agenda. The main reason for seizing power at the time they did was to thwart the peace process that had gained momentum since the November 1988 agreement between Colonel John Garang and Mohammed Osman al-Mirghani. Al-Mirghani, the leader of the second largest government party at the time, the Democratic Unionist party (DUP), had brokered a deal with the south, an agreement that was scheduled for ratification by a national constitution conference on 4 July 1989, only four days after the NIF coup. The new military regime was not going to allow a peaceful end to the war unless it could dictate terms to the south.

Having made its position clear on the two most divisive issues, religion and politics, the NIF regime proceeded to pay lip service to the idea of a negotiated peace while also making every effort to achieve a military victory. From day one, they set about altering the nature of the Sudanese army to ensure not only its military victory in the south but also the Islamic nature of its rule throughout the country. An Islamic militia was organized whose purposes were to prosecute an Islamic *jihad* (holy war) in southern Sudan and to protect the Islamic revolution in northern Sudan. Tens of thousands of young men and young women were recruited into the militia. Anyone in the country who did not ascribe to Islamic fundamentalist ideals was forced to do so. Since the June 1989 coup, although effective as forces of state terror in the north, the Islamic militias, by the regime's own admission and despite considerable loss of life, have failed in their holy mission to defeat the SPLA and enforce Islamicization of the south.

Four failed negotiations

If the repetition of an act could ensure success, the present Islamic fundamentalist regime and the SPLA would have achieved peace in Sudan by now. In the years since taking power in June 1989, the regime and the SPLA have held four sessions of peace talks and all of them have come to nought. Only two months after assuming power, the regime called for direct negotiations with the SPLA. The first encounter was organized in Addis Ababa in August 1989. Despite the niceties put out after the meeting, it was clear that the parties were not negotiating; rather, each was assessing how determined the other was in the pursuit of war. Before his delegation went to Addis Ababa, General al-Bashir made a public statement in Khartoum that he was sure his regime was going to achieve peace with the SPLA. He said that he and Colonel Garang were soldiers and that each would know how serious the other was because as soldiers they shared a common language. The only common language known to soldiers, of course, is the language of war. The message was clear. It did not need elaborating, but it was elaborated nonetheless, as the proceedings of the Addis Ababa meetings indicate.

The leader of the regime's delegation to this first round of talks and of all the peace conferences with the SPLA, the maverick Colonel Mohammed el-Amin el-Khalifa, put it simply: "We have come to listen to the case of our brothers from the south and to offer them our solution to it." This was not a situation in which there was anything to be discussed or negotiated about the system of government for Sudan. The regime had already made it clear what was on offer – Islamic fundamentalist rule or more fighting. The south could speak for what it wanted only within this framework. General considerations of what was needed for Sudan as a whole were not on the agenda. In the event, Addis Ababa failed; so did Nairobi in December of the same year, 1989; two further sessions at the Nigerian capital of Abuja in 1992 and 1993 also achieved little on the road to peace. A third round at Abuja, which would be their fifth meeting, was being planned at the time of writing.

What is at stake

In Addis, Nairobi and twice in Abuja, the SPLA and the regime failed to advance the negotiations because neither side trusted the other and therefore no serious discussion could develop. Mistrust between the north and south is a general problem; it has not just arisen with the Islamic fundamentalists but is at the heart of the Sudanese conflict. Even when agreement does occur it is eventually destroyed by mistrust, as happened with the 1972 agreement which ended the 1955–72 civil war. The engrained feeling in the north is that the south will not be satisfied with what the north offers and will want the ultimate: a separate and independent state of its own. To ensure that this will not happen, no northern political party or leadership is prepared to concede anything approaching equality to the south. Most northerners seem to believe that the south must remain part of Sudan, but that southerners must accept that they are not the equal of northerners, and that the north must remain in control of the country. They simply refuse to believe that southerners can take the fate of the country as a whole as seriously as they do themselves. Prejudice and mistrust run very deep indeed.

John Garang's call for a "New Sudan" of equal opportunities and responsibilities for all its nationalities is, to many northern Sudanese, as bad as a call by some southerners for separation. How can John Garang, a southerner, think that he and his kind can be the the equal of the Arabs? There are endless anecdotes that portray the deep racism that characterizes the northern view of the south, but in deference to brevity, two will suffice. A typical Arab northern Sudanese, who cannot bring himself to accept the frequently repeated slogan of the SPLA that they want to liberate the whole country and create a New Sudan, once remarked angrily: "Whom does John Garang want to liberate?" Another said, after the SPLA captured Kurmuk in Blue Nile province in December 1987 and was threatening to bring war deeper into the north: "How can John Garang, the naked Dinka from the cattle camp, think that he can rule Sudan?" The speaker was a primary schoolteacher who may very well not have gone beyond primary education himself, for often primary school-leavers are trained to teach at the same level. John Garang is not only an accomplished military officer, who has earned his present rank of colonel while an officer in the Sudanese national army, he is also an accomplished academic who holds a doctorate in economics. Some would say he is over-qualified for any job, but to this simple northern Sudanese he remains a southerner and thus a "naked Dinka from the cattle camp". These attitudes reveal what is at the heart of the Sudanese conflict: unadulterated racism with its usual components of prejudice and stereotyping. The religious element that now appears to dominate the political disagreement in Sudan is nothing more than an excuse for the north to perpetuate its long-standing racist, Arab rule over the country.

As I have said, these attitudes are not new. In the years immediately after independence, the first prime minister of Sudan, Ismail el-Azhari, put the matter starkly enough when he said: "This is an Arab country. It will remain an Arab country. Those who do not like it are free to leave it and go to wherever they like." This reflected the view of most northern Sudanese in the 1950s. Things do change slightly over time: by now, there are undoubtedly a number of northerners who would consider that statement awkward or in bad taste. For one thing, millions of southerners have left the south and are now living either in northern Sudan or in neighbouring countries. Indeed, southerners have established that Sudan belongs as much to them as it does to the northerners, that it is as much a black African country as it is an Arab country. Times have also changed to the point that racism in South Africa and elsewhere in the world has become something of a liability for those who make it an overt policy. As a result, religion became a convenient substitute to mask the racism of the northerners in Sudan, because the underlying attitudes have not changed. The Islamic fundamentalists use the rôle of Islam as an excuse with which to disguise Arab racism. The apparent debate about the rôle of Islam in the politics of Sudan today is basically about Arab domination of the Sudanese state and not a genuine religious call of duty. This is how the religious conflict in Sudan should be understood.

The future

The way out of the present crisis in Sudan still lies some time in the future. What follows here is inevitably a personal view. First, I do not believe that southern Sudan should ever reach a settlement with the present Islamic fundamentalist regime. This regime does not believe in democracy. As southern Sudanese, the only chance we have of ever being truly equal to the northern Sudanese in a united country is to insist on democracy. We do have a chance to influence matters with our parliamentary weight. We even have a chance of having a government of our own choice, if we work hand in hand with leaders from the other marginalized areas of the country who, like us, crave equal opportunities in their own country.

Secondly, this is a military regime that is, in fact, extremist by any standards. It has repressed all the people of Sudan. To reach an agreement with such a regime would be to condone their policies and absolve them of their crimes. In every aspect of the issues that divide us from the north –

politics, religion, economics, culture and power – this regime stands on the extreme right of anyone else in the north. They represent a minority view, at most 10 per cent of the north. It is not possible to reach a compromise with these people since Islam is their only political agenda, the excuse for their seizure of power and for the terrible repression that has followed.

Thirdly, the south should never again seek to reach an agreement just with the government of the day, especially if that government came to power through military force rather than national consensus. The south should seek an agreement on the future of Sudan with all the political parties in the country – those in power and those who are not as well. The present regime is military and extremist and it has declared all other political parties and forces to be illegal. The south cannot afford to legitimize the present state of affairs by coming to any form of agreement with it.

Furthermore, in practical terms, an agreement with the present regime could not last. It could not stand the test of history, given the crimes of this regime. Those who come to power after the regime is finally overthrown will be entitled to consider whatever arrangements the regime made during its period of power as illegal, including any agreement it might have made with the south. After all, southerners have made agreements with governments and parties before and none have lasted. Like the Nimeiri government before them, the present regime wants an agreement with the south that will consolidate its hold there and thereby allow it to concentrate on tightening its repressive hold on the north. One hopes that the south has learned from past experience and that it will not again allow itself to be used by a dictatorship to strengthen itself until such time when it chooses to throw all agreements overboard, as Nimeiri did.

What the country now needs is to rid itself of the present regime, to restore democracy and then to finalize an all-Sudanese agreement in which all the political forces in the country take part. It is already clear that an all-Sudanese agreement has begun to take shape during the summer of 1993 in the form of the discussions that have taken place within the opposition National Democratic Alliance (NDA).

However, it is not possible, as yet, to talk with much confidence of a future programme based on an agreement with northern Sudanese political forces, especially those who now form the NDA. Most of these parties have been tried and tested many times before in Sudanese politics, both in power and in opposition. One of the real tragedies of Sudan is that the country has plenty of clever politicians but no true statesmen. These politicians are unfortunately best known for their lack of word of honour and their lack of seriousness of intention. The widespread belief is that one's word, given while in opposition, cannot be considered binding once one is in government. A politician is expected to break his word of honour as long as he can provide an intelligent sounding explanation. This practice has so discredited politicians across the political spectrum in the country that agreements and commitments have become meaningless. This unhappy situation is compounded by the fact that it is virtually impossible to find a political leader in northern Sudan today in whom the whole country, south and north, might have confidence. In spite of all this bad experience, or perhaps in part because of it, it is still conceivable, because it is so urgently necessary, that the NDA could make a difference.

No rôle in politics for Islam

What the alliance needs to do is to consolidate its present charter, together with all the recently concluded documents on aspects of public life such as the economy, power sharing, the system of government and cultural diversity. It has taken more than three years to finally agree that the future Sudanese state should have no rôle for religion in the politics of the country, but this problem has now been overcome. On this basis it is, at last, possible to reach an all-encompassing Sudanese agreement. Now is the time to finalize such an undertaking, far from power itself but in readiness for the assumption of power under the new agreement.

After signing the original National Charter binding the political parties of north and south, including the SPLA, under the NDA umbrella in 1990, there was disagreement on what the rôle of Islam in the future politics of Sudan should be. In April 1993, this issue was finally resolved in Nairobi. All the NDA parties agreed that Islam should play no institutional rôle in the future politics of the country, although the state would respect and promote religious freedom and equality. There is still some room for concern that the traditional political parties of the north, especially the Umma Party and the Democratic Unionist Party (DUP), whose popular bases are religious sects and who have been committed in the past to some form of Islamic agenda, will continue to abide by the Nairobi agreement. But these two parties were not only signatories to the Nairobi agreement and to the NDA Charter, they were indeed the co-sponsors of both. And, given their own bitter experiences in the past, i.e. the failures that they both encountered when they were in power as a result of sticking to an Islamic agenda, there is every indication that they will honour their new agreements within the NDA in future. If that is the case, and it is certainly the one way forward that offers hope, what the alliance needs to do is to quickly convene an all-party constitutional conference at which this advance is consolidated and the NDA Charter and documents are put into constitutional form. This could be ratified in the future as the new national constitution of Sudan at a national constitutional conference, once the present regime has been overthrown and a new transitional democratic government put in its place. After all, the political groupings in the NDA represent a vast majority of the Sudanese people; whatever they support now is likely to gain the support of the Sudanese masses.

The parties under the NDA no longer need to behave as parties of the north and the south at the constitutional conference if they agree on a draft national constitution in advance. They merely need to present the document they now agree upon as the NDA proposal. In this way a practice will be established which begins to change ingrained and unproductive ways of thinking of the past and can contribute towards making matters simpler for the future.

Even though the NDA has now agreed on a framework that represents significant progress towards addressing what needs to be resolved in Sudan for the future, it is by no means certain that serious clashes will not erupt on the details of what has already been agreed. For instance, while the NDA seems to accept a liberal form of decentralization, it is not clear what powers will be considered adequate for the provinces, the regions or the federal states and what powers should remain in the centre. Should we start by allowing the regions to choose what powers they need to ensure equitable political and economic development and leave the rest of the powers in the centre; or do we begin from the currently contested premiss that all power belongs to the centre and that the centre alone can delegate powers to the regions? I am more in favour of the former. These are important matters on which agreement could break down in a country where the operative word is mistrust.

In addition, there is the pervasive issue of internal security arrangements. Southern Sudan is unlikely to accept any kind of power-sharing or system of government that does not allow it to retain its own army and to be totally in charge of its own internal security. Since independence in 1955, the south has lost almost two million of its people at the hands of a "national" army which has acted as an army of occupation. Given such experience, no one should blame the south for insisting that it wants its own army, or at least some kind of internal security arrangement that does not permit the army of the north to intervene in the internal affairs of the south.

The north, of course, is very suspicious about what the south might do with its power given half a chance. Northerners believe that the south seeks every opportunity to break away from the north and that the only way to ensure that this does not occur is for the north to maintain a strong military and security presence in the south, to thwart any such attempts and to maintain the union by force. Given the north's record in the south, the suspicion is neither unfounded nor unreasonable. The problem with this argument or suspicion is that it makes the north the perpetual policeman of the south. Who would want to maintain so unnatural a union?

"Guarantee any agreement"

There is also the entirely different issue of guarantees for the future for any agreement so far reached between the north and the south. Here again, the past presents dismal precedents. How can anyone, especially a southern Sudanese, have confidence that the same northern Sudan that has dishonoured so many agreements with the south will now abide by whatever will be agreed for the future? What water-tight guarantees can be incorporated into an agreement of this type that will not be broken by a willing offender once he has the power to do so with impunity? The north has a long and shameful history of unilateral betrayals, of broken agreements with the south – 1947, 1952, 1955, 1957, 1965 and 1983.

In 1947, the north promised that it would accelerate the political, economic and social development of the south in order to bring it to the level of the north, as a basis for national integration between the two parts of the country leading up to self-government and national independence. They completely failed to honour this agreement.

In 1952, northern Sudanese politicians stole away from their southern Sudanese colleagues and members of parliament to Cairo, where they signed the self-government agreement with the British and Egyptian condominium powers. That agreement provided for a transitional period of self-government during which the power of the state would be transferred to the Sudanese from the colonial authorities. It provided for the immediate Sudanization of the government in which northern Sudanese took over power from the colonial authorities. No southerners were offered any of the more than 800 jobs that were Sudanized, though there were southerners who would have qualified for these jobs. This exclusion, and the harshness of the northern administration in the south, as the new masters of Sudan took over from the British, gave rise to the 1955 mutiny which sparked the first 17-year-long civil war.

In December 1955, four months into the mutiny in the south, the southern Sudanese members of parliament refused to vote for the most important motion in the life of the country, which called on the British and the Egyptian colonial powers to hand over power to Sudan as an independent state on 1 January 1956, unless the parliament also promised that it would grant the south a federal relationship with the north after independence. The north promised that, once independence was achieved, federation would be considered. On the strength of that promise, the south voted for a resolution on 19 December 1955 on the declaration of independence. Once again, the north failed to honour its pledge. Federation was said to have been considered and rejected, without discussions with the south, because the north regarded it as unsuitable for Sudan.

In 1965, after the overthrow of the country's first military regime, the transitional government of Prime Minister Sir El Khatim El Khalifa convened a round table conference to negotiate a political solution to the civil war in the south. After 15 days of serious deliberations, the conference was adjourned to give its 12-man committee six months to work out recommendations to be presented at the next round of talks. The conference was never reconvened, and the resolutions of its 12-man committee were neither considered nor implemented. The north announced that political circumstances had changed and there was no longer any need to reconvene the conference or implement its resolutions. The circumstances that had changed in the country amounted to the fact that the north had by now held parliamentary elections without the participation of the south. The new government declared that it was going to end the civil war by military means and therefore it was no longer necessary to seek any political solutions. Naturally, the war did not end and further hundreds of thousands of innocent southern Sudanese lives were lost as a result.

In March 1972, the then military regime of General Nimeiri took the recommendations of the 1965 round table conference and presented them to the south as a self-government package. The south agreed and the war ended. Ten years of peace ensued for the whole country, and accelerated economic development began to take effect in the north. Even though there was hardly any development in the south following the end of the war, in the interest of peace alone, the people of the south preferred to be patient and wait. In 1983, Nimeiri dissolved the autonomy of the south because he did not want to meet the south's demand that it should share in the increased economic development. He also imposed Islamic rule on the whole country. The current civil war soon broke out.

Mediating the peace

In conclusion, hardly anything said here can be taken as an indication that settlement of the current civil war in Sudan is imminent. It will take the cooperative efforts of all concerned, the sincere determination of the international community and a great deal hard work to achieve a peace settlement. It should be clear too that, given the bitter experiences of the past nearly forty years, the Sudanese alone are not capable of finding a lasting solution to their problems. They need help from the international community in the form of advice, mediation, supervision and monitoring of any settlement. The real question is: given some very appreciable changes taking place in the world today, is the international community prepared to go an extra mile to settle the war in Sudan? It is a question very much in the air at present, and the answer may well provide the key to what will happen in Sudan.

Some recent developments in the international political arena may serve as useful guidelines to what the international community can do in Sudan. Elsewhere in Africa, the UN is involved in Mozambique in a peace mediation rôle; in Angola, the UN still has a direct rôle in working out a settlement of the war and creating a viable and acceptable political system for the country; we have also seen what the UN is attempting to do in Somalia. These are all civil war situations.

Elsewhere in the world, the UN is in the process of restoring democratically elected government in Cambodia and is still actively monitoring and supervising the process of a return to normality and democracy in El Salvador. These are situations in which a sitting government has not been required to give up power in order for the international community to reestablish democracy and the rule of law. All that is required is for the sitting government to co-operate, or be made to co-operate, in the process.

A possible settlement for Sudan, however, could take the shape of a new system of multi-party democratic government based on a secular constitution with considerable powers allocated to the regions or federal states. For southern Sudan, the new constitution would need to guarantee that internal security of their area is left in the hands of southern Sudanese, controlled and administered by them. It is almost inconceivable to imagine a settlement for the south in which the central government in Khartoum, even if it was controlled by southerners, would have any security powers over the south.

The reality, however, must be respected: that the overwhelming feeling in the south is one of absolutely no confidence in any system of government that emanates from Khartoum. Most southerners would like to see as much control as possible of their own affairs remaining in their own hands; they want to see a system that severely limits any interference with the affairs of the south by the centre.

It would be unrealistic, too, for the north to ignore the separatist feelings in the south. Separation can, however, be massaged and mollified by a strong system of decentralization such as a strong federation. Today confederation seems to be the bottom line for most southerners, who see it as the best way of ensuring that the country will remain unified geographically, while allowing the south to enjoy a high degree of autonomy without interference by the north.

Most southern Sudanese believe that the northern attitude to confederation today is exactly what it was to federation yesterday. In the early years of the southern political struggle for equality with the north, those southerners who called for a federal arrangement were persecuted. One of the southern leaders, the late Ezbon Mundiri, was sentenced to 20 years in prison for running and winning an election in the south in 1957 on a federation ticket. Northerners knew quite well that federation was not the same thing as separation, but they dishonestly and deliberately argued that the two were indistinguishable. Both were outlawed, and anyone who called for either federation or separation was a criminal. Nowadays, northern Sudanese all accept federation as a just system of government, but even so, they are not yet prepared to grant truly federal powers to the south. The urge to control the south is simply too strong in the north for a genuine solution to emerge in purely Sudanese negotiations. It is therefore crucial for the international community to assume the full rôle of mediator and supervisor of whatever will be finally agreed between northern and southern Sudanese.

Finally, if satisfactory negotiations are brought about and successfully concluded – and I trust that I have demonstrated that there is indeed enough room for successful negotiations to be achieved – it will be important that whatever is agreed upon should be implemented during a fixed transitional period. At the end of the transitional period, the people of southern Sudan should be asked in a popular referendum to confirm their satisfaction with both the agreement and its implementation during the transitional period. So much has happened to the people of the south at the hands of the central government in Khartoum in the nearly forty years since independence that it is imperative that they should have the final say over their future. Whether or not that say will leave them still part of a united Sudan or give them a separate and independent state, it would be totally wrong to deny the people this most important and inalienable right to self-determination.

CHAPTER EIGHT

Sudan's political future

CHARLES GURDON

Introduction

No "expert" or "analyst" likes to be proved wrong, and most cringe at the thought that their inaccurate forecasts will return to haunt them in years to come. There was the case of the academic who spent three years or more preparing a PhD thesis on Ghanian politics which was based on the argument that someone like Flight Lieutenant Jerry Rawlings could never again come to power. Apparently it was just about to be, or had only just been, submitted when Rawlings returned to power and the thesis required an extensive rewrite. Similarly, there were very few experts who believed that an Islamic revolution could ever sweep the Shah from power in Iran.

The consequence of this fear of being proved wrong is timidity and an unwillingness by all but the most foolhardy analysts to make any bold and unequivocal forecasts about what they believe is going to happen in a particular country. While most are prepared to *say* what they think, comparatively few are prepared to commit it to print for the fear of looking foolish.

Although it may be a risk, and might leave many future hostages to fortune, this chapter is an honest attempt to provide a personal interpretation of what I believe will happen to Sudan in the next five to ten years.

It is exceptionally difficult to forecast what will happen in Sudan and what the exact time frame for any likely scenario will be. In order to provide an accurate and comprehensive analysis, it is therefore essential to add numerous caveats to each and every potential scenario. Consequently, while trying neither to dilute nor to obfuscate the predictions, it is important to remember the caveats that qualify almost each and every sentence. I am sure that I will be accused of political bias and, while I have little faith in any of Sudan's current political or military leaders, it has to be admitted that I believe that the National Islamic Front (NIF)-dominated Islamic fundamentalist regime in Khartoum today is by far the worst of a pretty lousy bunch of post-independence Sudanese governments.

The regime is potentially very weak

Superficially, it appears that the current regime, which, although officially led by president Lieutenant General Omar Hassan Ahmad al-Bashir, is actually dominated by the NIF, is in a very strong position. In northern Sudan its human rights record, which has been absolutely appalling by Sudanese standards, has succeeded in subjugating the civilian population and this has enabled it to implement its radical political and social changes. Amnesty International, Africa Watch and other internationally respected human rights organizations have catalogued a spiral of repression where the torture of political prisoners has become virtually routine and the number of extrajudicial executions has been steadily increasing.

The regime has emasculated the national army, which is a microcosm of Sudanese society, both by sacking or forcibly retiring most senior officers except its own supporters and by giving the army the impossible task of winning an outright military victory in the civil war in southern Sudan.

At the same time, it has created and heavily armed its own Popular Defence Force (PDF) militia to act as its spearhead against the non-Arab tribes of central and western Sudan. It has given the militias virtual *carte blanche* to raid and plunder non-Arab villages and there are widespread reports of them killing men, raping women and capturing women and children to be kept or sold as slaves in northern Sudan and further afield. The combination of ideological indoctrination and the material rewards that these raids bring are intended to ensure that, in the event of a crisis, the PDF and the other militias will owe their allegiance to the regime rather than to the country.

Meanwhile in southern Sudan the regime has been assisted by, but has also fermented, encouraged and prolonged, the extremely damaging internal split within the rebel Sudan People's Liberation Army (SPLA) which, in the space of year, totally reversed the military situation. Having been forced to retreat to only three major garrison towns in 1991, the army's 1992 dry season offensive succeeded in recapturing almost all of the small towns in southern Sudan including the headquarters of the SPLA which suffered a string of military defeats and defections.

Despite this apparent strength, however, the regime's position is actually far weaker than it might initially appear. In the south the army's very success has left it dangerously over-extended, and, although it lost significantly less territory in 1993 than it does in most rainy seasons, it has still proved very difficult to resupply all of the newly recaptured garrison towns. Without the internal splits the SPLA would undoubtedly have inflicted major losses on the army, and it could still do so. If the losses were particularly high this would lead to further discontent in the one national institution which, if it properly and secretly planned, could still overthrow the regime tomorrow.

The current economic crisis has been hidden from the world by the regime's vocal propaganda about Sudan finally being self-sufficient in wheat and by its starting, albeit in a very limited and uneconomic way, domestic oil production. It is, however, only too apparent to most Sudanese, and it is continuing to fuel the discontent amongst the majority of northern Sudanese. They are suffering from the effects of hyperinflation, the shortages of essential commodities and the worst petrol crisis in memory. At the same time, they can see the regime's rampant corruption and its creation of a new rich merchant class from amongst its own supporters. This has created a dangerous combination of despair and anger amongst many northern Sudanese who feel, or may soon feel, that they have nothing left to lose and will be prepared to take action against the regime.

A bloody change of regime

In the short term this could possibly result in either a successful coup attempt or another people's revolution like those in October 1964 and April 1985 which overthrew the Abboud and Nimeiri governments respectively. Despite the regime's paranoia and excessive security measures, which have included announcing a number of alleged coups as an excuse both to arrest known opponents and to flush out potential others, it will never be possible to prevent army plots and attempted *coups d'etat*. Similarly, an increasing number of civilians feel that they have nothing left to lose and are now prepared to risk the consequences, even if it means their death, of taking part in a general uprising.

The difference between past changes of government and the one that will eventually overthrow the current regime is that this time it will be far more bloody. In the past the army has recognized which way the political wind was blowing and has returned to barracks without firing a shot, and the new governments took few reprisals against the old regime. Although a number of former president Nimeiri's closest associates were put on trial after April 1985, there was more rhetoric than positive action against the majority of his ministers. This is probably because the Sudanese ruling class is comparatively small and, with a few honourable exceptions, almost all had compromised themselves in some way or another during Nimeiri's 16 years in power.

There is little or no doubt, however, that the next change of power will be very different. The National Islamic Front (NIF) is probably prepared to do anything, including killing hundreds of unarmed civilians, in order to stay in power. Its leaders recognize that this will be the last opportunity to create an Islamic republic in Sudan and that neither the Sudanese army nor the people will be prepared to forgive the NIF for actions and human rights abuses since June 1989. Even if the NIF leaders are saved from the lynch mob, unless they manage to escape into exile, many will undoubtedly receive very severe prison sentences. Consequently, having nothing to lose, they will almost certainly go down fighting and will take as many of their enemies with them as possible. There will almost certainly be pitched battles between the army units and militias who owe their position, and therefore their loyalty, to the regime, and the majority who want an end to the ruling theocracy and a return to Sudan's traditional tolerance and multiparty democracy.

Within five years

While the NIF's existing oppressive security measures and the likely ferocity of its response to any threat makes it very difficult to forecast exactly when there will be a successful coup or peoples' revolution, there is little doubt that the regime will be overthrown some time in the next five years. Although it could happen tomorrow, the most likely time will probably be in 1994. This is because the standard of living will continue to decline still further before the economic benefits of the regime's reform programme finally begin to bear fruit for the majority of the population. At the same time, Sudan's continuing international isolation, even amongst former allies such as Libya and Iran, can only exacerbate the economic crisis. By the *end* of 1994, however, the economy could be showing significant improvements, the opposition could be totally crushed, and the regime's position could be so powerful that it would be very difficult to dislodge.

Unless it is prepared to model itself on other isolated pariah military regimes such as Mynamar, I believe that the regime cannot survive and that it will be overthrown within the next few years. Most analysts underestimated its longevity because we failed to recognize that the June 1989 coup was not a random event but part of a very well organized and financed plan that the NIF had been hatching for years. Also, those of us who knew and loved Sudan did not want to believe that any government would abandon so completely the friendly tolerance for which the Sudanese are famous throughout the Middle East. Despite its brutal suppression of all perceived opponents, I know of no analyst who believes that the regime can survive in power for more than a few more years.

In five years' time, therefore, there will almost certainly be a new government which will probably involve a short-term return to the *status quo ante*. In other words, after a relatively short one- to two-year transitional period when Sudan will be ruled by a broad based coalition, there will be general elections, at least in northern Sudan, and the Umma Party and the Democratic Unionist Party (DUP) will once again dominate the political scene.

Within ten years or possibly even earlier, it is likely that the traditional political system, which they have dominated for more than a century, will fracture. New political parties and a younger generation of political leaders are likely to emerge as Sudan moves towards a modern political system with a clear separation of religion from politics.

Sudan: one or two states?

The most important caveat to this scenario, however, is the seemingly insoluble question of whether or not Sudan will remain a a unitary state. Following the 1991 collapse of the Mengistu regime in Ethiopia, the SPLA lost its most important external base which had acted as a refuge for southern civilians in general and the Dinkas in particular. Addis Ababa was the site of both its largest overseas office and its radio station, which was a vitally important propaganda weapon to counter the regime's lies and distortions. Mengistu's overthrow led to hundreds of thousands of southern civilians being forced back across the border into Upper Nile region where they faced both starvation and attacks by the Sudanese army.

This, in turn, was the catalyst or the final straw which led to the breakup of the SPLA. In August 1991 one faction, which is Nuer-dominated and based around the Upper Nile border town of Nasir, claimed that it had replaced Colonel John Garang as the leader of the SPLA. Members of this faction accused his Dinka-dominated leadership of human rights abuses and stated that his aim of a unified secular decentralized Sudan was an unrealistic goal and that southern Sudan should simply secede from the rest of the country.

Since then the rivalry between the Nasir faction and the Garang "loyalists" has escalated into a very bloody conflict in which there have been major atrocities committed by both sides. Indeed, in 1993 it is likely that more southern Sudanese were killed by fellow southerners than by the regime's army and militias. Despite attempts at reconciliation there are still major outstanding issues, including Garang's leadership, which have to be resolved, and the fragmentation of the SPLA has continued unabated.

More importantly, there is now a seemingly irreversible move in the south towards support for the idea of secession rather than continuing to achieve equality in a unified Sudan. Garang himself now appears to recognize that it is impossible to swim against this tide and he has therefore been making ambiguous statements in support of secession if the regime refuses, as it undoubtedly will, to compromise on the central issue of Islamic *shari'a* law. No matter which southern group or organization eventually comes to dominate the region, it is likely that it will have to take the population's growing demand for secession into consideration.

In addition, the NIF would almost certainly be prepared to sacrifice the south if this was the only way that it could create and maintain an Islamic republic in northern Sudan. The longer the current regime stays in power, therefore, the more likely is the breakup of the country. If, however, it were to be overthrown within the next two years, it is possible that the southerners would perhaps be prepared to give northern Sudan one final chance to prove that it was prepared to ensure that not only the south but also the other peripheral regions received a fair share of the economic and political cake.

An initial return to the status quo ante

The overthrow of the current regime within the next few years will obviously lead to a radical change in the political situation in Sudan. Islamic fundamentalism will be totally discredited and, although religion will retain an important place in the lives of most Sudanese and its rôle in society will still have to be debated, it will be many years before it once again dominates the political scene. The question that therefore has to be answered is: what and who will replace Islamic fundamentalism in the short and medium term?

Throughout the past century the Sudanese political scene has been dominated by two families which lead the largest Sufi Muslim *tariqas* (sects) and their respective political parties. The Ansar *tariqa*, which is led by the Mahdi's descendants, and its Umma Party has been counterbalanced by the equally strong Khatmiyya *tariqa*, which is led by the al-Mirghani family, and its Democratic Unionist Party (DUP). Although it no longer advocates actual unity, the DUP has long had close ties with Egypt and receives the majority of its support in northern and eastern Sudan while the more nationalist Umma Party has traditionally been strongest in central and western Sudan.

These two conservative traditional parties were able to win the majority of the votes in past elections because in rural northern Sudan whole villages are allied to one or other *tariqa*. There have, however, been a multitude of other political parties, including the secular Baathists and the Sudan Communist Party which at one time was Africa's largest communist party; ethnic and regional parties such as the Nuba-dominated Sudanese Nationalist Party and Nuba Mountain Union, the Beja Conference, Darfur Front and a host of southern Sudanese political parties. In addition, non-political trade unions and powerful professional organizations have long played an important rôle in promoting a modern secular political system.

Immediately after the overthrow of the NIF regime it is likely that there will be a broad based coalition which will include all of the major political parties except the NIF, together with representatives from the trade unions and professional organizations and, more importantly, unless it has already finally opted for secession, the SPLA. There will probably be a transitional period before general elections are held but there is no way of knowing how long this will last. Although the Umma Party and DUP would want the shortest possible transitional period, because they correctly believe that they would win any election, the other parties will probably insist that it will take much longer than a year to undo the damage caused by the NIF. They will also insist that there can be no return to the *status quo ante* and that the decentralization of the country must be enshrined in constitutional changes which will ensure that all of the peripheral regions, and not just the south, enjoy a large degree of political and economic autonomy and receive a fair share of the economic development budget.

Although they will pay lip service to the idea of these changes, both the Umma Party and the DUP will push for an early general election because they believe, probably correctly, that they will be the largest single parties and that they can then carve up power between them in a grand coalition. This is particularly important for the Umma and DUP leaders, Sadiq El Mahdi and Mohammed Osman al-Mirghani respectively, because they have already been almost totally discredited and this is undoubtedly their last chance at power.

Initially it can be expected that the Umma Party and the DUP will indeed win the general election after the transitional period and that a grand coalition government will be formed. The expected collapse of support for the NIF, which was centred on the urban-based petty traders and lower middle class, will probably benefit the DUP more than the previously larger Umma Party and the two parties will therefore probably win a similar number of seats. In five years' time, therefore, it can be expected that Sudan will superficially have returned to the *status quo anti* that existed in the period between the April 1986 general election and the June 1989 coup, albeit without a strong NIF presence.

The caveats

There are, however, three important caveats that should be borne in mind when considering the long-term future of the country: the rôle of the military, the fragmentation of the major northern parties, and the situation in southern Sudan.

The rôle of the army

In the event of a successful coup which replaces the current NIF regime, it is possible that the army would refuse to hand over power to a civilian government after a transitional period. After all, Sudan's longest-serving,

111

and arguably most successful, post-independence government was led by former president Colonel Jaffer Nimeiri (1969–85). After he came to power in a coup in May 1969 he banned all traditional political parties and created his own Sudanese Socialist Union (SSU) which was modelled on Egypt's ruling party. Furthermore, it could justifiably be argued that the civilian political parties have let Sudan down very badly on two occasions (1964–9 and 1986–9) and do not yet deserve another chance.

The reality, however, is that the army is a microcosm of Sudanese society and that the majority of its officers are therefore either Umma or DUP supporters while its men are predominantly from central, western and southern Sudan. At the same time, the anticipated collapse of the NIF and the general weakness of Sudan's left-wing parties means that there is no obvious alternative ideology for the army. More importantly, after the NIF's hard-line and ideologically motivated regime which banned all other political parties, the Sudanese people will not be prepared to accept the domination of the country by a single party or group and will insist on the return to a multi-party political system.

Fragmentation of the main political parties

As far as the northern political parties are concerned, it seems likely that the fragmentation of the once monolithic Umma Party and DUP will continue to accelerate in future years. There are already dissident elements in both parties which are highly critical of the leadership of Sadiq El Mahdi and Mohammed Osman al-Mirghani. While some of the criticism is personal, from potential leadership rivals, much of it is ideological, from those who want to strengthen or weaken the link between politics and religion. With the demise of the NIF it is possible that there will be a realignment of Sudan's right-wing religious conservative groups and that a new party might emerge which would include the rump of the NIF together with the Umma Party and DUP's more religious elements.

At the same time, the liberal wings of both parties have long advocated the separation of politics and religion and the creation of Western-style ideologically based left- and right-wing political parties. Once again, although the loyalties to the old parties will probably remain strong in their traditional rural strongholds, it is possible that such new urban-based parties could be formed in the comparatively near future. Certainly within ten years, and possibly a lot sooner, a new generation of political leaders could have emerged in northern Sudan as the dominance of the El Mahdi and al-Mirghani families is finally broken. Together with the inevitable strengthening of regional based parties, this is bound to accelerate the process of fragmentation in Sudanese politics.

The future leadership of southern Sudan

Whether it becomes an independent state or remains part of a united but decentralized Sudan, it can be expected that the southern leadership will also change in the relatively near future. Having been the undisputed southern leader in the period from the start of the second civil war in 1983 until Nimeiri's overthrow in April 1985, when he was hailed by many as the country's saviour, SPLA leader Colonel John Garang's authority has steadily declined for a number of reasons. These include: his refusal to end the war after Nimeiri had been overthrown; his autocratic personality; the human rights abuses committed against dissident elements with the SPLA; its domination by his own Dinka tribe; and his refusal to compromise over his aim of creating a secular, democratic and united Sudan rather than helping the south to secede. All of these factors eventually led to the 1991 rebellion by the Nasir faction and the consequent weakening and fragmentation of the SPLA. Too much blood has been spilt, and there have been too many atrocities committed by both sides, to allow an effective and lasting reconciliation.

As a result of these factors, it is likely that, no matter when or how the civil war ends, Garang's hold over the south will continue to weaken and, although he might remain an elder statesman, he will be eclipsed by a new leadership. Because of the numerical superiority of the Dinka tribe in the south, it is also unlikely that the Nasir faction leaders, Riak Machar and Dr Lam Akol, will ever be able to dominate the entire region.

Given the hostility between the various southern tribes, it would appear that there are a number of alternative scenarios. New leaders could emerge from amongst either the SPLA's military commanders or the southern civilian leadership; a respected southerner such as former national vice-president Abel Alier could be drafted in to act as a figurehead leader; or the south could be redivided into the three old provinces of Bahr El Ghazel, Upper Nile and Equatoria. Although the Dinka-dominated Bahr El Ghazel would be the most powerful of the three, the Nuer- and Shilluk-dominated Upper Nile would have control not only of the Jonglei Canal, if it is ever completed, but also of the country's largest oil reserves.

Conclusions

This chapter has attempted to provide a clear and unambiguous prediction of what is likely to happen in Sudan in the next five years. Although I may well be proved wrong, and there are numerous caveats that one can add, my conclusions are that the evidence points to the following scenario:

1. The NIF-dominated regime will be overthrown in 1994 following either a military coup and/or a general uprising caused by a demonstration sparking off widespread rioting.

2. There will follow an 18-month transitional period during which Sudan will be ruled by broad based coalition which will exclude the NIF. On the surface, the period will be dominated by efforts to produce a new constitution which will guarantee sufficient political decentralization to persuade not only the south but also the other peripheral regions to remain part of single unitary state. If it fails to do so then definitely the south, and possibly other regions, will indeed secede. In reality, the period will probably be dominated by the formation of new political parties and a general jockeying for power in the run-up to a general election.

3. In 1996 general elections will be held in northern and, if it has not already seceded, southern Sudan. Although the Umma Party and the DUP will win over half of the total votes, regional parties will win a larger share than in any previous election. An Umma-DUP grand coalition will probably be formed but will inevitably splinter at the first sign of a major problem.

4. Before the end of the century the Umma Party and the DUP will have fragmented into a conservative religious wing and a secular progressive wing. There will have been a general realignment of the political scene, which in the urban areas will be based on left versus right and secular versus religious, with far stronger ethnically based regional parties. None of the major players currently in the political arena will be in power, although one or two may be figurehead leaders of one or other political and/or religious movements.

5. With luck, Sudan will begin the 21st century in perhaps the same position as say India was until relatively recently. In other words, it will be a decentralized multi-party democracy ruled by a central government but with powerful and effectively autonomous state administrations which genuinely represent the interests of the regional populations. If this is not the case, then it is unlikely that Sudan will remain a unitary state and its self-serving politicians will have condemned its people to the endless misery caused by continual civil war.

Glossary of political groups

Ethiopia

EPDM Ethiopian People's Democratic Movement
EPLF Eritrean People's Liberation Front
EPRF Ethiopian People's Revolutionary Party
EPRDF Ethiopian People's Revolutionary Democratic Front
IFLO Islamic Front for the Liberation of Oromia
Meison All-Ethiopia Socialist Movement
MLLT Marxist–Leninst League of Tigray
OLF Oromo Liberation Front
OPDO Oromo People's Democratic Organization
PGE Provisional Government of Eritrea
TGE Transitional Government of Ethiopia
TPLF Tigrayan People's Liberation Front
WPE Worker's Party of Ethiopia
WSPLF Western Somali Liberation Front (Ethiopian group)

Somalia

SDA Somali Democratic Alliance
SDM Somali Democratic Movement
SLA Somali Liberation Army
SNA Somali National Alliance
SNF Somali National Front
SNL Somali National League
SNM Somali National Movement
SPM Somali Patriotic Movement
SSDF Somali Salvation Democratic Front
SSNM Southern Somali National Movement
SYL Somali Youth League
USC United Somali Congress
USF United Somali Front
USP United Somali Party

Sudan

DUP Democratic Unionist Party – the political party of the Khatimiya *tariqa* which is dominated by the al-Mirghani family.
NDA National Democratic Alliance – rather fractious opposition alliance which

includes the Umma Party, DUP, SPLA and other smaller parties.

NIF National Islamic Front – coalition of Islamic fundamentalist political parties, dominated by the Muslim Brotherhood, which planned the June 1989 coup and which currently runs the regime in all but name.

PDF Popular Defence Force – militia created by the regime to protect its Islamic fundamentalist revolution.

SCP Sudanese Communist Party.

SNM Sudanese National Party – predominantly Nuba opposition political party.

SPLA Sudanese People's Liberation Army – rebel army and main southern opposition movement.

SSU Sudanese Socialist Union – created by former president Nimeiri as sole legal political party between 1969 and 1985.

Umma Umma Party – political party of the Ansar *tariqa* which is dominated by the descendants of the Mahdi.

Tribes and regions

Beja Non-Arab indigenous tribe from the Red Sea Hills in northeast Sudan.

Darfur Name of region in western Sudan but literally "home or land of the Fur" who are a persecuted non-Arab tribe.

Dinka Largest tribe in southern Sudan.

Nasir The name of the town in the Upper Nile region which is used as short-hand for the predominantly Nuer group that broke away from Colonel John Garang's leadership of the SPLA in August 1991.

Nuba Non-Arab and mainly non-Muslim tribe from the Nuba mountains of Southern Kordofan in central Sudan.

Nuer Second largest tribe in southern Sudan.

tariqas Sufi Muslim religious orders or brotherhoods which dominate life and politics in northern Sudan.

Regional organizations

OAU Organization of African Unity

Somali clans

Clan families	Clans	Sub-clans
Darod (Ethiopia, Kenya and Somalia)	*Dolbuhunta* (Somaliland) *Majerteen* (NE Somalia) *Marehan* (NW Somalia) *Ogaden* (Ethiopia, Kenya and SW Somalia) *Warsengeli* (Somaliland)	
Digil (central southern Somalia)		
Dir (Djibouti/northern Somaliland)	*Gadabursi* (Ethiopia/Somliland/Djibouti) *Issa* (Ethiopia/Somaliland/Djibouti)	
Hawiye (central Somalia)	*Abgal* (Mogadishu)	Harti
	Habr Gidir (central Somalia)	Saad 'Ayr
	Hawadle (Mogadishu airport) *Murasade* (Mogadishu port)	Salabaan
Issaq (Somaliland)	*Arap* *Gerhajis*	Habr Yunis Eidagalla
	Habr Awal	Saad Musa Issa Musa
	Habr Jaalo	

Index

119